THE ORIENTAL INSTITUTE OF THE UNIVERSITY OF CHICAGO

ORIENTAL INSTITUTE COMMUNICATIONS · NO. 22

THE ORIENTAL INSTITUTE OF THE UNIVERSITY OF CHICAGO

ORIENTAL INSTITUTE COMMUNICATIONS · NO. 22

EXCAVATIONS AT NIPPUR
ELEVENTH SEASON

by
McGUIRE GIBSON

With Appendixes by
M. Civil, J. H. Johnson, and S. A. Kaufman

THE UNIVERSITY OF CHICAGO PRESS · CHICAGO & LONDON

International Standard Book Number: 0-226-62339-4
Library of Congress Catalog Card Number: 75-9054

THE UNIVERSITY OF CHICAGO PRESS, CHICAGO 60637
THE UNIVERSITY OF CHICAGO PRESS, Ltd., LONDON
© 1975 by The University of Chicago. All rights reserved.
Published 1975. Printed in the United States of America

CONTENTS

LIST OF ILLUSTRATIONS

LIST OF ABBREVIATIONS

ARMT   Archives royales de Mari [transcrites et traduites] (Paris, 1950——).

Hg.   Lexical series ḪAR.gud = *imrû* = *ballu,* published in *MSL* V—XI (Rome, 1957—74).

Hh.   Lexical series ḪAR.RA = *ḫubullu,* published in *MSL* V—XI (Rome, 1957—74).

JNES   Journal of Near Eastern Studies (Chicago, 1942——).

MSL   Materials for the Sumerian Lexicon. B. Landsberger, *et al.,* eds. (Rome, 1937——).

OMRO   Oudheidkundige Mededelingen uit het Rijksmuseum van Oudheden te Leiden. Niewe Reeks (Leiden, 1920——).

REC   F. Thureau-Dangin, Recherches sur l'origine de l'écriture cunéiforme (Paris, 1898).

TuM   Texte und Materialien der Frau Professor Hilprecht Collection of Babylonian Antiquities im Eigentum der Universität Jena (Berlin, 1932——).

UET   Ur Excavations; Texts. Publication of the Joint Expedition of the British Museum and of the Museum of the University of Pennsylvania to Mesopotamia (London, 1928).

ZAS   Zeitschrift für Aegyptische Sprache und Altertumskunde (Leipzig, 1863—1943; Berlin, 1954——).

In Memory of Saleh Hussayn Dakkhil,
a gifted pickman and an extraordinary
individual. He began digging with the
Institute at Khorsabad in 1929 and died at
Nippur on the night of February 14, 1973.

Preface

This preliminary report on the 1972/73 season at Nippur, Iraq, is a revival of "Oriental Institute Communications," a series that before World War II brought into print the findings from Institute expeditions. It is our intent, with such reports, to publish as soon as possible the basic information gained from each season's work. The format chosen is very different from that used in the old *OIC*'s, which were in fact more like final reports than preliminary ones. Here, we stress the raw data, relying on catalogues of objects, sheets of sherd drawings, and many photographs rather than interpretation of them. We present as much as can be given at this point in our analysis, rather than just the more attractive pieces. Admittedly, the material is undigested. Surely, some of our views on levels, significance of material, and the like, will change. But we think it better to present our findings for others to work with when it is fresh in our minds rather than wait for some final monograph years from now. As will be seen, our work this season was not final in any way. No operation was brought to a point where more answers were given than questions raised. In the main area of our work, we came upon what seems to be a complex of temples. The elucidation of that sequence of temples and the area nearby will take several seasons. To wait until the entire operation is complete is clearly less preferable than giving a yearly account. Stressing analyses and interpretations, the final report will focus upon the meaning of the information given in the preliminary reports.

The foregoing paragraph implies a continuing program of research at Nippur. With the building of a large, permanent expedition house in 1964, the Oriental Institute committed itself to such a program. Prior to that event, directors were almost every season given notice that the Nippur expedition was about to close. Having assumed the field directorship in 1972, I take the long term nature of the expedition as an opportunity to work on a group of specific problems, testing archeological and historical assumptions, and in other ways treating Nippur as a laboratory. It is hoped that we and others, such as Robert McC. Adams, who uses Nippur as a base for surveys and excavations in the Nippur area, may develop a regional program, putting Nippur in its environmental and cultural setting.

For the 1972/73 season, the Nippur staff was somewhat larger than usual. We had the good fortune to have Professor R. C. Haines, the former director of Nippur, and his wife Irene, at the site with us. They were both invaluable for their advice, their contribution of time and effort in the work, and in helping to train the staff, including the director, with kindness and diplomacy. It is hoped that the Haineses may return for future seasons, as their time and inclinations permit.

The rest of the staff consisted of the present writer as director; Sayyid Adnan Muhsin Jabber as representative of the Iraqi Directorate General of Antiquities; Miguel Civil as epigrapher and photographer; Douglas Kennedy, general supervisor and coordinator of pottery; John Sanders as architect and photographer; Charles Smith, Juris Zarins, Constance Piesinger, Vernon Grubisich, and Curtiss Brennan as site supervisors. Mary Brennan was indispensable in recording, cataloguing, and keeping the finds orderly. She also assisted in sorting and drawing sherds and in numerous other ways.

The site supervisors were in charge of specific squares, recording the work of trained pickmen as well as their own. WA 6−13 was recorded by Juris Zarins, Curtiss Brennan, and Constance Piesinger. WA 50c was the responsibility of Charles Smith. WB was supervised by Vernon Grubisich. All finds, especially the sherds, were the responsibility of the individuals in charge of squares. Douglas Kennedy was especially helpful in coordinating the recording and analysis of sherds from all locations.

The trained pickmen were a mixture of Sherqatis and local men. Khalaf Jasim was foreman. Other Sherqatis were Saleh Hussayn Dakkhil, Saleh Jasim, Hussayn Ali, Ali Hussayn, Saleh Hussayn Hameda, and Haswa Abdul Rahman. At the death of Saleh Hussayn Dakkhil, we hired his brother Muhammad Hussayn Dakkhil. The local pickmen were Abda Sadeh, Hakim Muhammad, Nassir Hussayn Rabat, Rahi Mutar, and Ghafil Ghanim. The skill of these men varied from excellent to fair, but the entire group was well above average. To Khalaf Jasim, the foreman, should go much of the credit for working out the tricky stratigraphy in our main operation, WA. His skill in organizing and handling men was essential to the success of the dig.

The rest of the Iraqi staff consisted of fifty local men, mostly of the Afak tribe.

Equipment consisted of the usual tools: the small pick, trowel, grapefruit knives, brushes, and the like. For removing the meters of deliberate Seleucid fill, it was thought justified to use large picks. Debris was removed with a small-gauge railroad.

Extensive collections of sherds, bones, soil, and carbon samples were made. The sherds from some of our operations have not been fully studied, having not been received in Chicago before this report was completed. We include sherd drawings whenever possible. The soil samples were in part collected by Dr. Peter Mehringer, of Washington State University.

For aid in the course of this season, we owe great debts of thanks to Dr. Isa Salman, Director General of Antiquities. Dr. Isa gave encouragement, cooperation, and understanding throughout the season. We also owe much to Sayyid Fuad Safar and the rest of the Directorate staff.

The expedition wishes to acknowledge the help of the Ford Foundation for traineeship grants, which supported three of the students. We also wish to thank Mr. Herbert Reutzel of the American University of Beirut for allowing us to rent a Landrover for the duration of the season.

The British School of Archaeology was most gracious throughout the campaign. We wish to thank Diana Kirkbride, Nicholas Postgate, and especially Theodora Newbould for all their help.

Mr. Lowrie and Mr. Main, of the American diplomatic mission in Baghdad, were also helpful to us in many ways. We were pleased to have them and others from the various diplomatic missions as visitors at Nippur. Also visiting with us for several days were Mrs. Elizabeth Tieken and Dr. and Mrs. John Livingood. It was a pleasure to repay these Institute members with our rustic brand of hospitality for their continued support.

Finally, I wish to thank Ms. Rose Diamond for supplying, in her usual way, unique insights into our work and novel interpretations of our results.

I

INTRODUCTION

After a pause of five years, the Oriental Institute resumed excavations at the city of Nippur, Iraq (Fig. 1), on December 20, 1972.[1] The season, which lasted until March 20, 1973, was the eleventh Institute campaign since 1948.

In the previous ten seasons, attention was concentrated upon the eastern half of the city, the sacred areas, and Tablet Hill (Fig. 2).[2] Logistical problems, such as a great mass of Parthian and other "late" material overlying earlier Babylonian remains, made it seem likely that results commensurate with time and expense would not be forthcoming from continued work in these locations. Investigation of the residential parts of the city might tell more about the special role of Nippur in Sumerian and Babylonian religion, as well as give information on the life of ordinary people in a sacred city.

Although Nippur was excavated extensively by the University of Pennsylvania (1889—1900) long before the Institute's involvement, the site is so large that little can yet be said about the growth and layout of the city. Even the city walls have not been adequately traced. It is hoped that the Institute's commitment to Nippur will continue to be a long-term one and that a concerted program of research can be carried out not only in uncovering specific buildings but in outlining the history of the city as a dynamic, growing, and changing entity.

As a first step in such a program, this season was devoted to the West Mound (Fig. 2), which is relatively undisturbed, although Pennsylvania did make extensive cuts in the southern tip and in an area where a large villa with a Court of Columns was found (Fig 3, Nos. IX—X, I).[3] Both these localities were seemingly of a secular nature and had levels that are of prime in-

---

1. For a report on the last season of work, see J. Knudstad, "A Preliminary Report on the 1966—67 Excavations at Nippur," *Sumer* XXIV (1968) 95—106.

2. See D. E. McCown and R. C. Haines, *Nippur* I: *Temple of Enlil, Scribal Quarter and Soundings* ("Oriental Institute Publications" LXXVIII [Chicago, 1967]), for publication of some of these findings. A second volume, *Nippur* II, is in press.

3. See J. P. Peters, *Nippur* (2 vols.; New York, 1897) II 172 ff. for the best published account of this building.

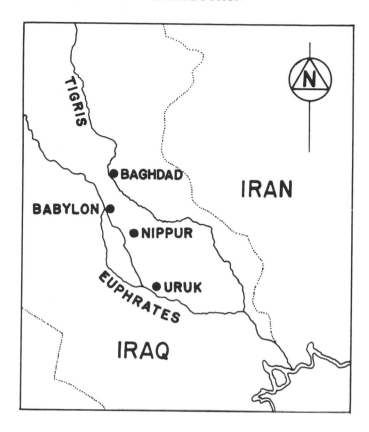

Fig. 1.—Map of southern Iraq

terest to the Institute staff. The area around the Court of Columns seemed especially attractive since it was in this vicinity that Pennsylvania found the famous Murashû archive, a family's business records dating to the Achaemenid Period, and several hundred Kassite (second millennium B.C.) administrative tablets.[4] The Kassite texts had been discovered by means of a tunnel dug below the villa, several meters west of the Court of Columns. Viewing of the area in 1964/65 had left me with the impression that the exact findspot of the tablets was still under a few meters of debris, but that the Court

---

4. *Ibid.,* p. 188 for a description of the finding of the Kassite tablets. Publication of some of these texts, mixed with other Kassite tablets from the southern end of the West Mound, was in *The Babylonian Expedition of the University of Pennsylvania,* Series A: *Cuneiform Texts* (ed. H. V. Hilprecht), Vols. XIV–XV (Philadelphia, 1906), XVII (Philadelphia, 1908). For the discovery of the Murashû archive, see H. V. Hilprecht, *Explorations in Bible Lands* (Philadelphia, 1903) pp. 408 ff. For a general study and a full bibliography on the Murashû tablets, see G. Cardascia, *Les Archives des Muraŝû, une famille d'hommes d'affaires babyloniens a l'époque perse (455–403 av. J.-C.)* (Paris, 1951).

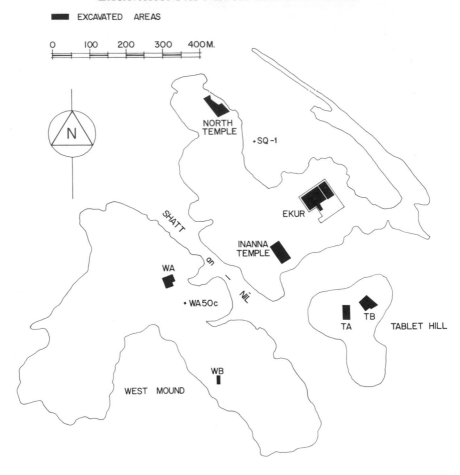

Fig. 2.—Plan of Nippur showing the work of the Oriental Institute
since 1948

proper was an open, large pit. Various published and unpublished Pennsylvania reports[5] seemed to indicate that even if we could not reach the locus of the tablets, we could touch upon Kassite levels in the pit, under the Court. There was, however, some inconsistency in the reports. The Kassite levels were variously described as being only a meter, more than two meters, and three meters below the Court of Columns, which was most probably a Seleucid construction.[6] Our season's work would, hopefully, resolve the problem of

5. Unpublished field notes and manuscripts were made available from the University Museum of the University of Pennsylvania with the assistance of Diane E. Taylor.

6. The dating of this building, which had been termed "Mycenaean" as well as Kassite and Parthian, has been discussed by E. J. Keall in "The Significance of Late Parthian Nippur" (Ph.D. diss., University of Michigan, 1970) pp. 52–53.

inconsistencies and yield remains of buildings or a building associated with those Kassite tablets, or at least give some notion of the time and effort needed to recover Kassite in this place.

As the season developed, plans were changed and expectations frustrated as well as rewarded. Devaluation of the dollar and major civic and religious holidays curtailed work to an extent. The weather, however, was more favorable than one could hope for, there being only four days lost to rain and sandstorms. A great deal of work was done, and the results in all operations were good.

In the Court of Columns area, called WA (West Mound, Operation A), a large grid of ten-meter squares was laid out. The entire pit left by Pennsylvania was cleared to undisturbed dirt, and four of the squares were taken down in places as deep as five meters below the Court of Columns.

In order to obtain more quickly an idea of the strata below the Seleucid levels, we sank a stratigraphic pit (WA 50c) in a gully south of the Court of Columns. This small cut proved to be surprisingly rich in information and finds.

Farther to the south, we opened Trench WB, which was designed to step down a gully that appeared untouched by Pennsylvania. Since the surface of this slope was littered with hundreds of "Kassite goblet" sherds and it was near this place that Pennsylvania found another Kassite archive, we thought we had a good opportunity of reaching Kassite material quickly. As will be seen, this area proved to be, under the surface, very different from what was expected.

One final operation was carried out during the campaign. Dr. Peter J. Mehringer, an earth scientist, dug a 3 × 3 m. pit, designated SQ–1, in a low area northwest of the ziggurat in the eastern part of the city (Fig. 2). This pit was made in order to examine a gray layer that R. C. Haines said had been found in the SK soundings of 1951/52.[7] Haines had assumed at the time that the gray layer was marsh sediment. Mehringer sampled all layers of the pit for faunal and pollen studies. Publication of his results, which may be a record of the last six thousand years of environmental conditions at Nippur, will appear after complete analysis.

7. See McCown and Haines, *Nippur* I 156 f. for these soundings.

II

AREA WA

In February, 1919, H. R. Hall, on his way to work at Ur, visited Nippur and took a photograph of the "Parthian palace,"[1] which we referred to above as the villa with a Court of Columns. In the photograph, the baked-brick columns are much as they had been when exposed by the Pennsylvania Expedition in the 1890's. In the same year, James Henry Breasted and D. D. Luckenbill also took a series of photographs of Nippur, including the villa (Fig. 4A). Their photographs show the building in even better detail than Hall's had done. Sometime between that date and the beginning of the Oriental Institute's excavations in 1948, almost every baked brick was removed from this structure.[2] When we arrived in mid-December, 1972, to begin work (Fig. 4B), only a few crescent-shaped bricks lay scattered about the area. Not enough was left of the mud-brick walls of the building, as far as exposed by us, to relate them to the plan previously published (Fig. 5).[3] Further work in coming seasons will, we hope, make more precise the plan of the villa and the Court. It is clear from this season's findings, however, that Pennsylvania's plans were to a great extent conjectured, reconstructed, and in places wrong. In this report, we make no attempt to deal with the villa, leaving it for the final monograph.

The main area of WA is a large, rectangular cut, oriented approximately northeast by southwest. Along the southwestern edge of the pit there is a large area of sand dunes under which is the locus of the Kassite archive. Up to two meters of sand lay in the pit left by Pennsylvania, and our initial task was the removal of this accumulation. Beneath the sand, the surface was very uneven. Pennsylvania had cut a long, deep trench roughly east to west across the northern end of the area, and a shallower but wider trench

1. H. R. Hall, *A Season's Work at Ur* (London, 1930) p. 65. Hall reports that the local British political officer, Capt. Daly, had carried out restoration work on some columns of the building and had done similar work elsewhere at Nippur.

2. R. C. Haines saw no sign of columns when he came to Nippur for the first season (personal communication).

3. The most complete plan of the building is in Clarence S. Fisher, "The Mycenaean Palace at Nippur," *American Journal of Archaeology* VIII (1904) 431, Fig. 20.

through about the middle of the northeast-southwest axis (Fig. 6). Backfill in these cuts and in other smaller trenches was confusingly similar to deliberate filling done by Seleucid builders. In places, we found undisturbed walls and floors directly under the sand. In others, we could follow Pennsylvania's trenches down to four meters. Under these conditions, our excavation area was very irregular, difficult of access, and disorderly to the eye. Baulks were almost impossible to maintain, and we often found it necessary to abandon them and re-establish others, sometimes without relation to square divisions. In practice, the earth directly under walls became our baulks since we were under obligation to maintain as many walls as possible for restoration purposes. Only when deeper remains seemed to justify the removal of a structure could we demolish it and the "baulk." This set of circumstances made it more difficult to correlate floors or tamped earth surfaces in adjacent, but separate, areas. The maintenance of walls on high baulks also made the removal of debris very arduous, especially in squares in which meters of fill by Pennsylvania or the Seleucid builders allowed us to descend at a rapid rate. Baulks were, however, essential in working out the stratigraphy which, even without Pennsylvania's intervention and the ancient builder's excavating and filling, proved to be extremely difficult. After weeks of puzzlement, it became clear that the Pennsylvania reports of Kassite remains at varied depths were accurate. Area WA is at the edge of the Shatt an-Nīl, which was either the ancient Euphrates or a canal that bisected the city. In this location there was always a slope toward the river, with consequent erosion, dumping of debris, and digging out of small pits perhaps for the making of mud bricks or mortar. In the course of excavating in WA 12 and 13, levels that represented tamped earth surfaces would disappear, cut by ragged ancient holes, then reappear. It was only when we had reached house levels some 4 meters below the Court of Columns that we were able to reconstruct a sequence of revetments and structures related to a series of superimposed buildings at the southwestern edge of the excavation (Fig. 7). Thus far, there is evidence of at least four phases of these buildings. We have been able to uncover only a part of the outer, northeastern, niched and buttressed wall, a north corner, and a short stretch of the northwest wall, but there is evidence enough to say the buildings were temples. Strata associated with the various phases of the temples and the material above can be divided into six levels (Fig. 9).

LEVEL V, OLD BABYLONIAN PERIOD

The earliest level (V) is certainly in evidence in Rooms 1 and 2 of the temple (Fig. 10), at the lowest point of our excavations. Here, in the small space available for work, some bits of wall were discovered. Mud bricks in the walls were a size (22 × 16 × 7 cm.) that is possible for the Old Babylonian Period. An administrative tablet fragment, possibly of Old Babylonian date (Appendix A, No. 16), was found below Floor 12 in Room 2. Sherds (Fig. 39) found on and above Floor 12 were within the Old Babylonian range, or even earlier. We were not able to expose enough of the walls to judge if this lowest structure was built with the same plan as those above it, nor were we able to touch its outer face to ascertain if it was niched and buttressed. We are assuming that the building, with some shared wall lines, is a precursor of the niched and buttressed structure above. Found on Floor 12, in Room 2, were two excellent cylinder seals (Fig. 28:1, 2), perhaps heirlooms since they are of Akkadian date, and a broken stone axe inscribed with the name of a deity, probably a goddess (Fig. 28:3a, b). The inscription on this last item, combined with the niching and buttressing of the upper versions of the building, gives us the best indication of a sacred function for the structure. On Floor 10 were found two more Akkadian cylinder seals (Fig. 29:1, 2).

Outside the temple, to the northeast, the Old Babylonian phase is in- dicated by a whole jar and sherds found on floors associated with the build- ing marked *I* on Figure 10. Wall L, which runs directly under Wall K (Fig. 8) and must also run under Kassite Wall J, should prove to be Old Baby- lonian. Its mud bricks, measuring 24 × 16 × 9 cm., may be suited for that period. At Level V, 2, Wall I was rebuilt with slightly different alignments. Sherds from this floor and Level V, 1 may show a transition to the Kassite Period. An expansion of Wall L, in mud bricks measuring 30 × 30 × 10 cm., seems to have been done at Level V, 1 or IV, 3 and may have been the foundation for a basin.

LEVEL IVb, KASSITE PERIOD

The Kassite remains of the temple (Wall J and Floor 9 in Rooms 1 and 2, Fig. 9) are firmly fixed in time through the occurrence of some Kassite goblet sherds and many button bases (like those on Fig. 43), but especially through the discovery just below Floor 9 in Room 1 of a round school tablet (Appendix A, No. 18) dated to the Kassite Period. The mud bricks of Wall J are 24 × 16 × 7 cm.

Perhaps contemporary with Wall J are two stubs of wall in WA 7 (Walls AK, AP, Fig. 10), but until further digging is done in this square, the date cannot be definitely determined.

A lower part of a fragmentary wall (H, see Fig. 12) associated with Level IV, 2 is probably Kassite. See below for discussion of Wall H.

LEVEL IVa, LATE KASSITE OR MIDDLE BABYLONIAN

It is difficult to divide Level IV on the basis of sherds, since all floors yielded "Kassite" items, but we would suggest that with Level IV, 1 there was a restoration (Wall K, Fig. 11) following the lines of the Kassite temple. Wall K was built in a trench cut to about Level IV, 3 from Level IV, 1 (Fig. 9). A widening of the trench below Level III, 5 may indicate a Neo-Baby- lonian cut-and-fill operation along the same lines preparatory to the revet- ment wall (G) and fill behind it. We know that Wall K was later than Wall J and that in the restoration a solid mud-brick platform was laid down inside the rooms of the temple on or slightly above Floor 9. Floor 7, above the platform, seems to have been the only floor associated with the rebuilding.

The mud bricks in Wall K and the platform measure 30 × 30 × 10 cm. Similar bricks in Walls AJ, AL, AM, and AN in WA 7 (Fig. 11) lead us to propose that these walls were contemporary with Wall K. Wall AJ seems to be the face of another niched and buttressed building lying to the northwest. Perhaps we have touched upon a complex of temples, rather than just the one series on the southwestern edge of our cut. Work in future seasons may prove these walls to be earlier than Wall K, but they seem to fit best with it.

Also suggested as contemporary with Wall K are the walls in WA 13 (marked *P* on Fig. 11). Because we were obliged to leave one wall of a later structure (Achaemenid Chapel) standing, we were unable to work out by strata the relationship of these walls with Wall K. It is clear, however, that the material associated with these walls (e.g., Fig. 46) is most similar to that from Level IV. This particular problem will be worked on in subsequent seasons.

At present, Wall F cannot certainly be shown to have originated at Level IV, 1, when we think Wall K was built. It seems more likely that Wall F was a Neo-Babylonian wall laid in a trench from Level III, 5. The ashes against its northeast face were later than the wall. I am assuming that there was a slope from Wall K to Wall P, and that in preparation for the setting in of Wall F, some floors of Level IV were cut away.

The trenches for Walls F and K definitely cut Wall H (Figs. 14–15), which is associated with Level IV, 1, as well as Level IV, 2. This wall, though badly preserved and probably not well built originally, furnishes us with a *terminus post quem* for the building of Wall K. The lower phase of the wall, clearly Kassite, had a horizontal drain (Fig. 14) that was situated just below and served Level IV, 2. On top of this wall was a rebuilding with a drain that lay just below Level IV, 1, that is, the stratum at which we think Wall K was built. One of the baked bricks of the upper drain had a stamp of Kadashman-Enlil II (1275–1269 B.C.). The brick was meant to be used at the Ekur and was probably reused in the drain some time after the date of this king.

Probably contemporary with Wall K was a badly preserved wall (AE) in WA 7.

LEVEL III, NEO-BABYLONIAN

With Level III, 5, this area (Fig. 13) witnessed rebuilding on a well planned, grand scale. Inside Rooms 1 and 2, above Floor 7, there was about a meter of deliberate fill, consisting mainly of mud bricks and straw-tempered plaster that probably came from the Level IV*a–b* temples. On the outside, over rubble from the Level IV buildings, the builders put in a retaining wall (G, Figs. 15, 16). The area behind Wall G was packed with mud bricks.

Some time later, from Level III, 4, Wall F seems to have been built into a cut, as previously described. This wall turned a corner and apparently continued to the northeast. The mud bricks in it were laid in a disorderly fashion and were on a scale (27 × 27 × 11 cm. to as large as 35 × 28 × 15 cm.) that is unusual before the Parthian Period (Fig. 17).

The debris between Level III, 3 and III, 2a seems to be the result of deliberate filling over some time. The floor marked Level III, 2a, a creamy plaster that runs to and up the temple face, would seem to be the first surface associated with actual use of this version of the temple. Subsequently, a repair was made to the building, as is evidenced by a line of mud bricks and a new plastering, the "red line" (Fig. 9).

Level III, 1 seems to mark a definite destruction, perhaps in preparation for a temple restoration that was never completed. Walls E_1 and E_2 appear to be revetment walls that would have been constructed as part of that renovation.

Before turning from the Neo-Babylonian version of the temple, we should mention that we have uncovered more of it than of its predecessors (Figs. 13, 18, 19). There are curious features in its construction. The buttresses are far from regular, and there are intentional plastered-over niches that appear to the casual eye to be merely cuts. We have no explanation for such features.

Within the Neo-Babylonian temple, on Floor 4, were found a baked-clay plaque fragment with the lower legs of a mythical beast (Fig. 29:4) and a bronze hoof (Fig. 29:3), probably from an almost life-sized statue of a calf or from some piece of furniture.

In Level III outside the temple, several fragments of horse-and-rider figurines were found (11 N 95, 105, 133, Fig. 33:4—5). The provenience for these pieces reinforces the evidence presented by McCown and Haines[4] for the pre-Achaemenid popularity of such objects.

Wall AD (Fig. 13), which lies under Wall C, is composed of mud bricks 31 × 31 × 12 cm., the same size as those in Wall D, the temple proper, and Wall G. The similarity in brick size, plus the elevation of Wall AD, leads to the conclusion that it was also Neo-Babylonian. There were at least five Neo-Babylonian tablets (Appendix A, Nos. 23—25, 29, 30) found below the level of Wall AD in WA 7—8, but they cannot be used to date the wall. Pennsylvania trenches cut into and disturbed Seleucid fill that had been put in with Wall C, which in turn cut into fill for Wall AD. There was no undisturbed material in WA 7—8 until the elevation of Wall AE. Even at that depth there were ancient cuts through walls and floors.

LEVEL II, ACHAEMENID

Directly upon the Neo-Babylonian temple wall (D) a small, unbuttressed wall (B_3) was constructed (Fig. 9). Mud bricks in this wall measured 31 × 31 × 12 cm., the same as in Wall D. In what had been Room 2 of the earlier

4. *Nippur* I 91—92.

temples, at this level called Locus 2, a mud-brick platform underlay part of Floor 2. The debris on and above this floor was not distinctive enough to ensure firm dating. Wall B₃, however, was contemporary with Level II, Floors 1 and 2a outside. On Level II, 1 rest the badly preserved remains of a small chapel (Figs. 20, 21). This structure was destroyed by pits in the southeastern part, and it lost an entire room on the northwest when the foundation cut was made for Wall C.

The chapel was basically tripartite in plan, with a central room entered on the short side and flanked originally by a room on either side. The entrance was recessed, and there were buttresses on the outside. There was an unexplainable niche and projection in the outer part of the back wall, near Wall C. Inside the main room, there was no partition into cella and antecella, although a slightly worn baked-brick door socket alongside the northwest wall, about midway into the room, may have supported a swinging screen of light material that shielded the cult statue. An ancient cut destroyed part of the back inner wall, but it is probable that there was a niche here for such a statue. The recesses in this room were asymmetrical, as were the doorways into the subsidiary rooms.

Between the main entrance and the door to the southeast, on Level II, Floor 1, two items (11 N 61, 62) were found against the wall. One is an Egyptian stele showing the boy Horus, holding snakes and scorpions (Fig. 34:3). An Egyptian hieroglyphic inscription on the reverse and sides is an incantation against these two animals (see Appendix B, below). The second item is a fragment of an alabaster bowl (Fig. 34:4). These items, and the sherds from the chapel, allow a dating to the Achaemenid Period.

Although the chapel was shortlived, being demolished at Level I, 7 and covered with a thick deposit of reddish, clayey debris, the structure with the wall we have called B₃ continued into Level I, 6 (Fig. 9). Sunk into Level I, 6, in the eastern corner of our working area, was a basin lined with whitish mud plaster (Fig. 22). This basin may prove to have been nothing more than a pit used in construction, but it seems more formal than that. Complete excavation may reveal its function.

The next higher surface, Level I, 5, was almost featureless. To the northeast was a baked-brick pavement with no preserved walls nearby. On the southwest, Wall B₃ was still in existence. Parallel to this wall was a long cut that sloped toward a vertical drain (Fig. 22, south corner of Locus 1). Alongside this cut was a small, square bench of mud brick covered with a thick coat of plaster. A glance at the plan (Fig. 22) would lead one to assume that this bench was contemporary with the wall just south of it, since the two were more or less aligned. Yet, this wall, although it did rest in part on Level I, 5 (Fig. 9), was of later date, being set in from Level I, 3.

On Level I, 4, also to be associated with Wall B₃, the plastered bench was enlarged and set at a different angle. The long horizontal pit was no longer in use, but the vertical drain was enclosed within a box made of baked and unbaked bricks set against Wall B₃.

LEVEL I, SELEUCID

At Level I, 3, we found definite Seleucid material. The sequence of construction in this phase is as follows: On the stub of Wall B_3, another wall, B_2, was set with a slightly different alignment. The mud bricks in this wall measured 31 × 31 × 12 cm., a size met with in several earlier walls. A doorway led from Locus 2 to an annex, Locus 1, which seems to have been built a short time after Wall B_2, since its walls abutted but did not bond with the main wall. An attempt was made to tie in the annex with Wall B_2 by cutting the foundation trench below the level of the main wall and inserting one mud brick under it (Fig. 9). A doorway from Locus 1 to the outdoors was indicated by the remnant of a sill.

The well preserved doorway into Locus 2 still retained its plaster. In fact, we were able to discern a narrowing of this doorway that resulted when a course of mud brick was added inside either side of the opening and replastered (Fig. 23A). At the same time the doorway was changed, the earlier sill of baked bricks was plastered over and faced, on the outer edge, with a row of small baked bricks set on edge.

Inside Locus 2 there was evidence of two floors to match the sills. The earlier one, Floor 1, was a compact, beaten earth floor with two slightly raised platforms at either end of the room. A mud-brick partition dividing the room was furnished with a baked-brick door socket. A later floor, Floor O, was found upon the platforms and is to be associated with the renovation in the doorway. Little information was gained from Floor O.

Locus 2 had several interesting features and yielded important dating items. Under the floors in three places were small holes (Caches 1–3) cut down into the mud-brick platform of the Achaemenid level. In one hole, located in the doorway connecting the two halves of the room, were two small bowls set one on top of another (Figs. 23B, 36:3 and 4). In the corner made by the junction of the partition and Wall B_2 was a second similar cache (Fig. 36:5, 6). The third cache (Fig. 36:7), inside the partitioned space, had only one bowl. These caches might have been foundation offerings, but there was nothing found in the lower bowls. I would suggest that these caches might have been for safekeeping of valuables. A fourth cache (Fig. 36:8) was found sunk from Floor O into the platform in the east corner of the room.

Objects in the room on Floor 1 were a bowl and a plumb bob (11 N 69, 70, Fig. 36:2), found in the northwestern end, near the platform. In the same place, but a few centimeters under the floor, was a badly worn bronze coin (11 N 174, Fig. 36:1). This coin is definitely Seleucid and is an issue of either Antiochus IV (175–163 B.C.) or Demetrius I (162–150 B.C.). Therefore, Floor 1 in Locus 2, Wall B_2, and the annex built at Level I, 3 cannot be earlier than these dates.

Outside the buildings there were some features to be noted. There were some ovoid pits, lined and built up with mud plaster. These pits, or bins, were sunk in from Level I, 3. Some ashes were found in one of the pits, but the others were relatively clean. Their function may have been constructional, as mortar or plaster mixing pits for the building of Walls B_1 and B_2.

LATER LEVELS IN WA

The sequence that we can reconstruct for the bits of walling around the
edges of WA is very tentative. Wall C, the massive L-shaped wall that bi-
sects our working area, is definitely later than our Level I but earlier than
the Court of Columns. Wall C was part of a foundation for some very large
building that lies under the debris at the north. The construction of the wall
is interesting (Figs. 24, 25). A pit was dug as large as the building to be
constructed. The outline of the building was laid out in a single line of mud
bricks and the inside area filled to the height of that course. Then the second
course was laid with two lines of bricks and the slightly diminished inner
area filled in. A third course of three bricks was laid, filled in, and so forth
until the desired wall width was reached. The method of construction called
for much labor and huge quantities of fill (which came from some uninha-
bited area of the mound) but allowed effort and expense to be saved on
brick-making. Carl Haines described this procedure and indicated that it was
carried on into Parthian times, for example, in the Inanna Temple.

The Court of Columns was built later than Wall C. Wall A_1, on the southwestern edge of our cut, some fragments of mud-brick wall, A_2, on the southeast (Fig. 22), and a pavement of baked bricks on the northwest (Fig. 6, WA
2–3) seem to be part of that structure.

Parthian brickwork in the faces of the Pennsylvania pit rests at various
levels above the Court of Columns.

OBJECTS AND SHERDS FROM WA 7–13

The critical objects from this operation have been mentioned in passing.
In the catalogue that follows, all registered objects are given by level, with
the lowest, earliest material first. As far as possible, items are shown in
photograph or drawing (Figs. 28–38), especially those that were well stra-
tified and distinctive or comparable with dated objects.

The sherds from this operation have been more fully analyzed and drawn
than those from the other areas, and a selection of them has been presented
(Figs. 39–52) in order to allow an evaluation of our dating of levels. On the
figures, diameters are given wherever an estimate was possible. The set of
numbers accompanying each sherd is a variation on a descriptive code
worked out by H. J. Nissen.[5] An explanation of the code can be found on the
page facing Figure 39.

Figures 39 to 41 show sherds from the small sounding made inside Room
2 of the Neo-Babylonian temple. Floors 11 and 12 yielded sherds that were
not particularly distinctive but were clearly Old Babylonian or earlier. Note
for example the comb-incised sherd and carinated-rimmed bowls from Floor
12 (Fig. 39), which we date Isin-Larsa. On Floor 9 we found numerous
sherds from Kassite vessels. We do not illustrate these, but they are of the
same type as the sherds shown in Figure 43, upper left, and Figure 44, upper

5. See R. McC. Adams and H. J. Nissen, *The Uruk Countryside* (Chicago, 1972) p. 107.

left. Floors 4 and 3 within the temple have been dated Neo-Babylonian and later, and the appearance of black-painted sherds (Fig. 41, upper right) should be linked to contemporary glazed wares with similar designs.[6]

In the building found above the temple, and dated to the Seleucid era, some fine-ware bowls and wares with impressed designs should be noted (Fig. 41).

The sherds from the area outside the temple (WA 12—13) were much more numerous and furnished a better set of diagnostic markers. One can see a transition in Level V from thin-walled goblets to solid footed ones (Fig. 42, upper left and lower left), that is, from Old Babylonian to Kassite shapes. In Level IV, the prevalence of Kassite types (Figs. 43—44) is to be noted. There seems to have been a progression toward taller and thinner forms as time went on. The stamp-impressed sherds in this level (Fig. 43) are probably holdovers from Isin-Larsa.[7] In Level III (Figs. 47—48) the goblets continue but diminish in number, while bowls with flaring rims make an appearance. Also in this level and in Level II handles were an important feature. Level II, which we date Achaemenid in part, was marked by impressed wares. It should be mentioned that the leaf-shaped impressions normally thought of as Achaemenid were nonexistent in this level but were numerous in Level I, which we date Seleucid (Fig. 51).

The occurrence of glazed wares is very interesting. We have a few glazed sherds and glazed horse figurines from as low down as Level IV, that is, Kassite. The glaze in this level was light green. In Level III, contemporary with the Neo-Babylonian temple, there was a continuation of glazing but no marked increase in number, and the color varied from light green to blue-green. With Level I, there was a sharp difference in glazing. The most frequent color was white, but a yellow glaze was also in evidence. Only a few sherds were green glazed. The dramatic shift from green to white and yellow glazes was also apparent in WA 50c, as will be seen. We have been allowed to bring from Iraq a selection of glazed sherds and hope that chemical and other analyses will allow us to say something more definitive on the history of early glazing.

---

6. See McCown and Haines, *Nippur* I, Pl. 100:9.
7. See *ibid.*, Pl. 88:12—13.

Fig. 3.—Plan of the West Mound of Nippur, from Peters, *Nippur* II, following p. 172. The Court of Columns, our Area WA, is marked *I*. Area WB is approximately on the knoll north of F in the southern end of the mound.

Fig. 4.—*A*. The Court of Columns in 1920. Photograph taken by D. D. Luckenbill, from the northeast. *B*. Area WA, the site of the Court of Columns, seen from the east before excavation, December, 1972.

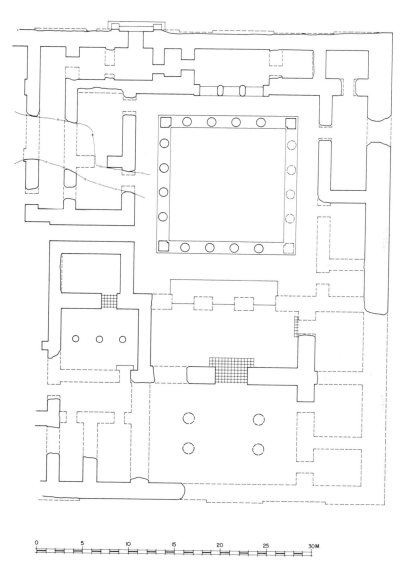

Fig. 5.—Plan of the Court of Columns, adapted from C. Fisher, in *American Journal of Archaeology* VIII (1904) 431, Fig. 20

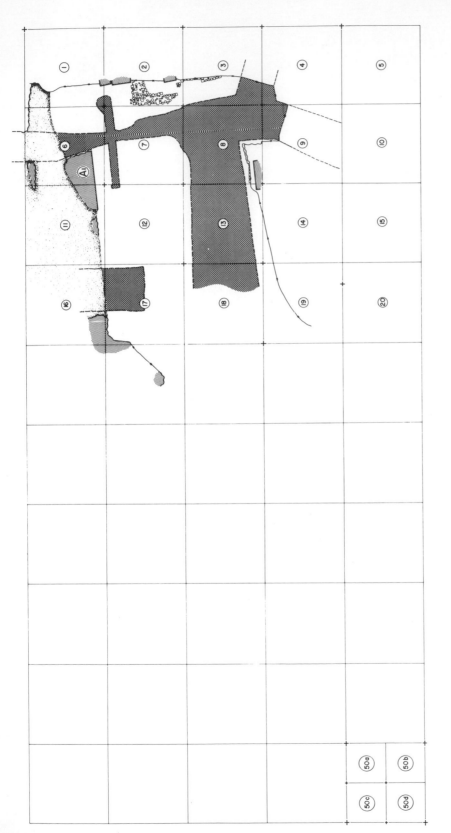

Fig. 6.—Plan of squares in Area WA, with Seleucid walls, bits of the Court of Columns, and Pennsylvania cuts indicated

SELEUCID WALL

SAND

PENNSYLVANIA CUT

40 M

30

20

10

0

Fig. 7.—The outer walls of the niched and buttressed buildings on the southwestern edge of WA with dune above, from the northeast.

Fig. 8.—Area WA, Square 12, Wall L running under Wall K, from the east

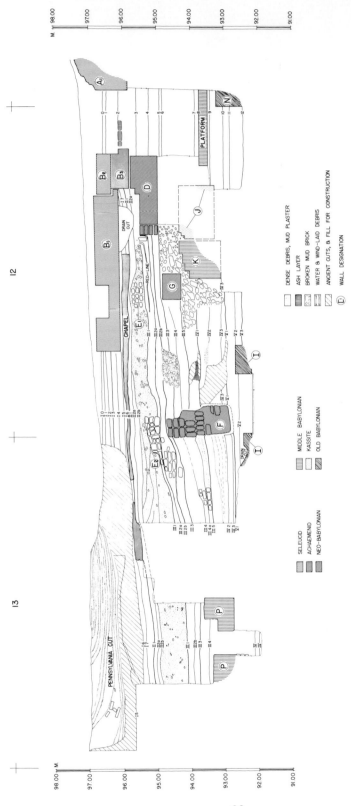

Fig. 9.—Master section C-C of Area WA

22

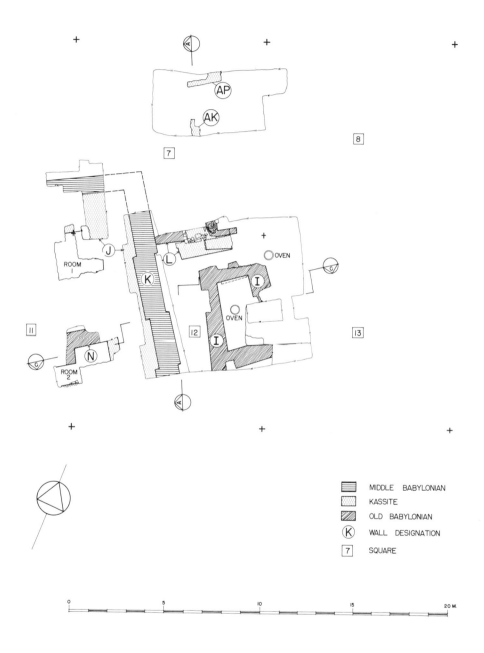

Fig. 10.—Plan of WA, Levels V and IV*a*

23

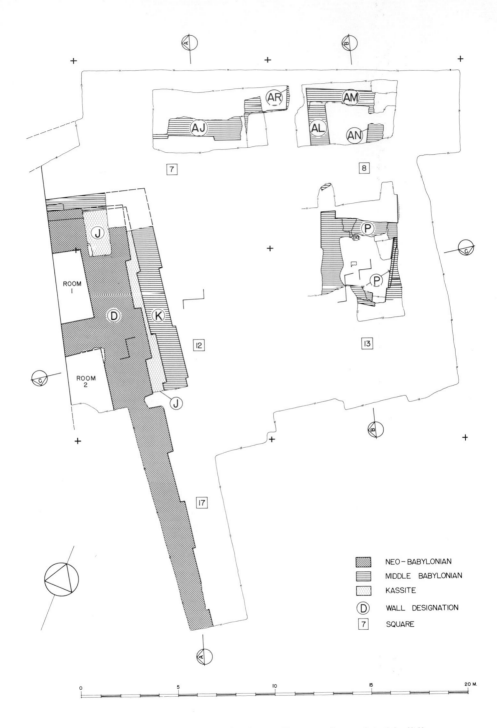

Fig. 11.—Plan of WA, Level IV*b*, lower floors and associated buildings

NEO-BABYLONIAN
MIDDLE BABYLONIAN
KASSITE
Ⓓ WALL DESIGNATION
7 SQUARE

0   5   10   5   20 M.

24

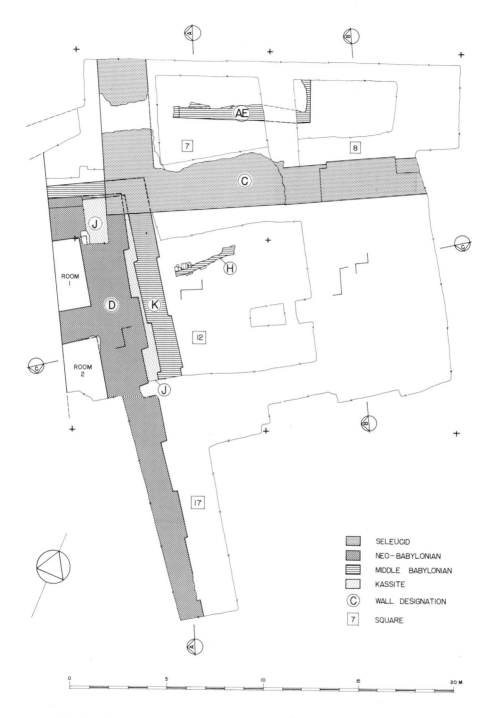

ROOM 1

ROOM 2

SELEUCID
NEO-BABYLONIAN
MIDDLE BABYLONIAN
KASSITE
Ⓒ   WALL DESIGNATION
7   SQUARE

0   5   10   15   20 M.

Fig. 12.—Plan of WA, Level IV*b*, upper floors and associated buildings

25

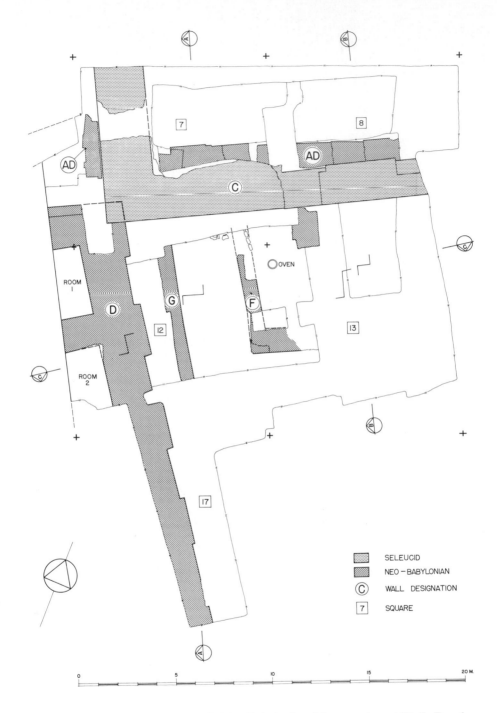

Fig. 13.—Plan of WA, Level III, Neo-Babylonian. Note revetment Walls F and G. Slope down to the ancient river or canal bank is to the right.

26

Fig. 14.—Area WA, Square 12, from northeast, Wall I with two baked-brick drains through it. To the right, structure L and Level IV, 2, which runs over the lower drain visible at the left end of Wall I. The upper drain is above and to the right of the lower one but not so clear.

Fig. 15.—Area WA, Square 12, from northeast, revetment Wall G in front of the Neo-Babylonian temple wall. Wall F in left foreground.

Fig. 16.—Area WA, Square 12, southeast baulk showing niched and buttressed walls of Kassite and Middle Babylonian times on the right. Revetment Wall G at the top of the baulk, with mud-brick fill under it.

Fig. 17.—Area WA, Square 12, revetment Wall F from the west. Note the irregular construction of very large mud bricks.

Fig. 18.—General view of Area WA from the northeast, with niched and buttressed Neo-Babylonian outer wall. The large wall in the foreground is Seleucid Wall C, that to the right under the dune is Seleucid Wall A.

Fig. 19.—General view of Area WA from the southwest, showing niched and buttressed Neo-Babylonian wall as far as its north corner near Seleucid Wall C.

29

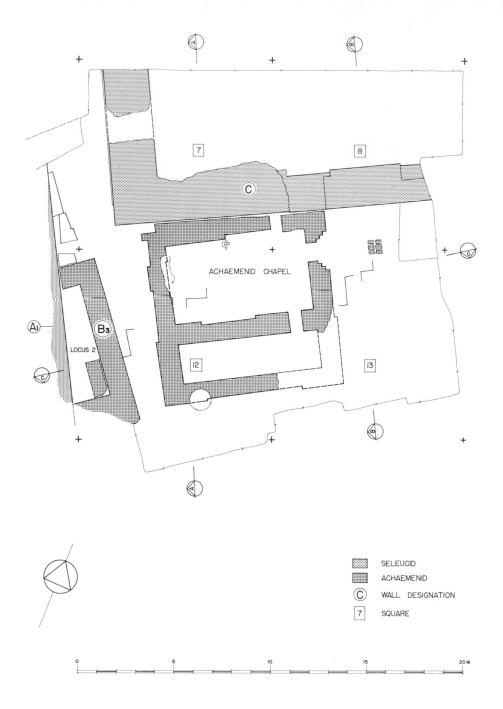

SELEUCID
ACHAEMENID
ⓒ WALL DESIGNATION
7 SQUARE

Fig. 20.—Plan of WA, Level II, Achaemenid, including small chapel.

30

Fig. 21.—General view of Area WA, Level II, with the Achaemenid Chapel from the east. Note the altar in front of the doorway.

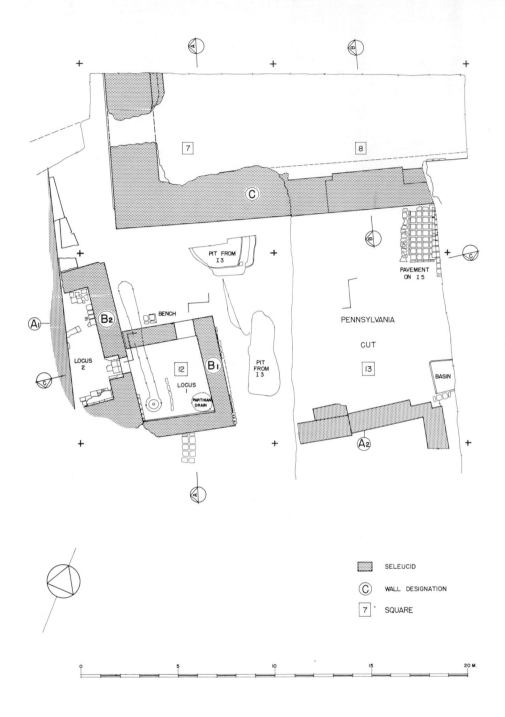

7

8

C

PIT FROM
I 3

PAVEMENT
ON I 5

B₂

BENCH

LOCUS
2

A₁

C

12

B₁

LOCUS
1

PARTHIAN
DRAIN

PIT
FROM
I 3

PENNSYLVANIA

CUT

13

BASIN

A₂

SELEUCID

C   WALL DESIGNATION

7   SQUARE

0   5   10   15   20 M.

Fig. 22.—Plan of WA, Level I, Seleucid

A

B

Fig. 23.—Area WA, Level I, Locus 2, from the west, detail of the doorway showing rebuilding (*A*) and from the southeast, showing two caches cut down from Floor 1 (*B*).

Fig. 24.—Area WA, Seleucid Wall C, with Pennsylvania cut through it from the northeast. Note the stepped construction of the foundation.

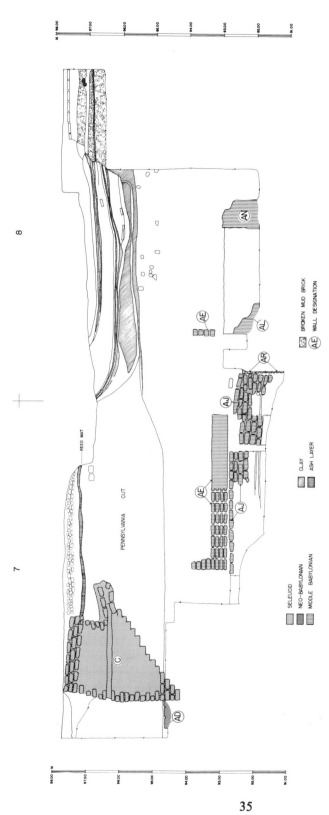

Fig. 25.—Section of Area WA, Squares 7–8, northwest profile. Wall C construction on the left, Pennsylvania trench and later wind-blown fill on the right.

35

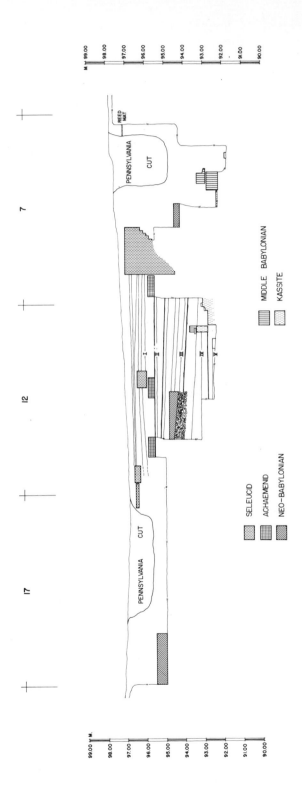

Fig. 26.—Section A-A of Area WA

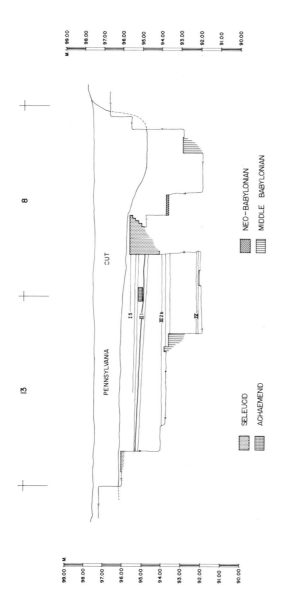

Fig. 27.–Section B-B of Area WA

CATALOGUE OF OBJECTS
BY LOCUS AND LEVEL IN WA

From inside Temple Rooms 1–2

FIELD NUMBER	DESCRIPTION*	ILLUSTRATION
11 N 179	Speckled black stone cylinder seal with presentation scene; Akkadian; 3.5 h., 2.2 dm.; WA 12, Room 2, Floor 12	Fig. 28:1
11 N 180	Black stone cylinder seal with contest scene; Akkadian; 3.4 h., 2.25 dm.; WA 12, Room 2, Floor 12	Fig. 28:2
11 N 191	Fragmentary green stone axe; couchant lion; cuneiform inscription: "Property of Nin[. . .]"; 5.7 h., 4.9 l., 2.3 w.; WA 12, Room 2, Floor 12	Fig. 28:3*a–b*
11 N 172	Shell cylinder seal; hero protecting animals; transitional ED III–Akkadian; 4.1 h., 2.65 dm.; WA 12, Room 2, Floor 10	Fig. 29:1
11 N 177	Black stone cylinder seal; contest scene; Akkadian; 4.0 h., 2.75 dm.; WA 12, Room 2, Floor 10	Fig. 29:2
11 N 171	Diamond-shaped gray stone bead; 4.7 l., 4.0 w.; WA 12, Room 2, Floor 9	— —
11 N 101	Copper bull's hoof; 3.2 h., 9.3 l., 7.2 w.; WA 12, Room 1, Floor 4	Fig. 29:3
11 N 102	Fragmentary baked-clay plaque; legs of a mythological creature; 5.9 h., 6.1 w., 1.8 th.; WA 12, Room 1, Floor 4	Fig. 29:4

From area enclosed by Wall P in WA 8–13
Level IV

11 N 149	Fragmentary baked-clay horse figurine; green glaze; 3.0 h., 5.5 l., 2.6 w.	Fig. 30:1
11 N 150	Fragmentary baked-clay figurine, bearded man with vase; 7.5 h., 3.2 w., 2.5 th.	Fig. 30:2
11 N 173	Fragment of brown stone cylinder seal with inscription; OB or later; 1.9 h., 1.3 dm.	Fig. 30:3
11 N 181	Fragmentary pottery bowl with pointed bottom of fine reddish ware, reddish slip with incised lines; 7.7 h., 10.6 rim dm.	Fig. 30:4
11 N 182	Fragmentary platter with indentations inside; grater(?); 10.0 h., 33.5 dm.; coarse buff ware, reddish slip	Fig. 30:5
11 N 183	Fragmentary horse figurine; green glaze; 5.4 h., 5.5 l., 2.5 w.	Fig. 30:6

From above Wall P in WA 8–13
Level III

11 N 63	Fragmentary baked-clay bearded male figurine; 7.1 h., 5.1 w., 2.0 th.; see *Nippur* I, Pls. 128:2, 129:2.	Fig. 31:1

*Measurements are in centimeters.

38

FIELD NUMBER	DESCRIPTION	ILLUSTRATION
11 N 125	Fragmentary female figurine nursing child; 5.4 h., 3.7 w., 3.95 th.	Fig. 31:2
11 N 144	Fragmentary baked-clay mold, for making *puzuzu*(?) amulets; 2.9 h., 4.2 w., 1.8 th.	Fig. 31:3

From WA 8, 12, 13 (exclusive of temple and area associated with Wall P)
Level V

11 N 186	Fragmentary pottery jar; medium fine, chaff-tempered, grayish-buff ware with cream slip, black paint around rim; 30.0 h., 20.0 dm.; see *Nippur I*, Pl. 90:15; WA 12, Level V, inside room made by Wall I, lowest floor	Fig. 32:1
11 N 184	Two fragments of one black stone vessel; joinable; 3.3 h.; WA 13, southwest end, Level V, 2	——

Level IV

11 N 153	Fragmentary female figurine; 7.3 h., 2.6 w., 2.5 th.; WA 13, southwest end, Level IV, 3	Fig. 33:1
11 N 146	Fragmentary "Kassite goblet"; medium coarse, chaff-tempered buff ware with a cream slip; 27.4 h., 9.7 dm.; WA 12, Level IV, 2	Fig. 32:2
11 N 194	Fragmentary "Kassite goblet"; medium coarse, chaff-tempered reddish ware with a cream slip; 34.5 h., 10.6 dm.; WA 12–13, Level IV, 2	Fig. 32:3
11 N 147	Fragmentary horse figurine; green glaze; 2.5 h., 5.2 l., 2.4 w.; WA 12, Level IV, 1	Fig. 33:2
11 N 148	Fragmentary female figurine; 3.8 h., 3.0 w., 2.8 th.; WA 12–13, southeastern part, Level IV, 1	Fig. 33:3

Level III

11 N 133	Fragmentary rider from baked-clay horse-and-rider figurine; 5.5 h., 2.1 w.; WA 12, Level III, 5	Fig. 33:4
11 N 136	Damaged pottery lamp; medium coarse, chaff-tempered greenish-buff ware, no slip; 6.0 h., 16.0 l.; WA 12–13, southeastern part, Level III, 5	Fig. 34:1
11 N 107	Fragmentary baked-clay plaque, female(?); 6.6 h., 4.6 w., 3.3 th.; WA 12, Level III, 3	——
11 N 105	Fragmentary baked-clay horse-and-rider figurine; traces of red and black paint on horse's back and rider's legs; 5.0 h., 8.5 l., 4.1 w.; WA 12, Level III, *2a*	Fig. 33:5
11 N 95	Fragmentary baked-clay horse-and-rider figurine; 8.6 h., 10.5 l., 3.5 w.; WA 12, Level III, 1–2	——
11 N 143	Fragmentary four-legged pottery incense burner; very coarse, chaff-tempered, greenish-buff ware with a greenish slip; incised and impressed decorations; 11.0 h.; WA 12, Level III, 1, near temple wall	Fig. 34:2

FIELD NUMBER	DESCRIPTION	ILLUSTRATION
11 N 145	Fragmentary baked-clay animal figurine; 5.0 h., 5.6 l., 2.5 w.; WA 13, Level III, 1	——
11 N 100	Fragmentary rider from baked-clay horse-and-rider figurine; 7.2 h., 3.6 w., 3.25 th.; WA 12, Level III	Fig. 33:6
11 N 185	Fragment of rider from horse-and-rider figurine; 9.0 h., 3.3 w., 2.3 th.; WA 12, Level III, 1, directly under southwestern wall of Achaemenid Chapel	Fig. 33:7

Level II

11 N 108	Fragment of baked-clay horse figurine; 6.2 h., 1.9 w., 4.3 th.; WA 8–13, Level II, 2 under main room of Achaemenid Chapel	——
11 N 134	Rectangular black stone plumb bob or whetstone; 8.4 l., 1.9 w., 1.3 th.; WA 12–13, under southeastern room of Achaemenid Chapel, in a cut from Level II, 2	——
11 N 195	Fragmentary baked-clay plaque; bearded man in profile; OB; 5.8 h., 4.0 w., 1.5 th.; WA 12–13, under southeastern room of Achaemenid Chapel, in cut from Level II, 2	Fig. 33:8
11 N 61	White stone stele; Egyptian hieroglyphs on reverse and edges; Horus as a child holding snakes and scorpions, surmounted by face of Bes on obverse; see Appendix B for discussion; 8.8 h., 8.3 w., 3.1 th.; WA 13, in main room of Achaemenid Chapel, against northeast wall, Level II, 1	Fig. 34:3
11 N 62	Three fragments of a white stone bowl; 3.6 h., 14.0 dm.; see Schmidt, *Persepolis* II (Chicago, 1957) Pl. 62:1, 2; same locus as 11 N 61	Fig. 34:4
11 N 64	Fragmentary baked-clay nude female figurine; pubic triangle indicated by hatching; 7.1 h., 4.1 w., 1.1 th.; see *Nippur* I, Pl. 122:4, 13 for type; WA 12, inside main room of Achaemenid Chapel, Level II, 1	——
11 N 67	Flat, circular bead of white composite material, possibly glazed frit; deteriorated; 3.5 dm., 1.65 th.; WA 12–13, inside main room of Achaemenid Chapel above Level II, 1	——
11 N 68	Fragmentary white stone weight(?), with hole drilled in one end; 6.9 h., 3.55 w.; WA 13, in main room of Achaemenid Chapel, Level II, 1	——
11 N 65	Fragmentary baked-clay model bed with plain surface; 9.6 l., 6.0 w.; WA 12, Achaemenid Chapel, southeastern room, Level II, 1	——
11 N 135	Copper pin; 6.1 l., 0.15 dm.; WA 12, Achaemenid Chapel, southeastern room, Level II, 1	——

FIELD NUMBER	DESCRIPTION	ILLUSTRATION
Level I		
11 N 71	Copper pendant; flattened sphere with loop; 1.35 h., 0.9 w., 0.5 th.; WA 13, fill above Achaemenid Chapel, Level I, 7	— —
11 N 72	Polished black stone pendant; 1.95 h., 1.6 w., 0.45 th.; WA 13, cut from Level I, 7	— —
11 N 73	Baked-clay mold with plant design; 2.7 h., 2.3 w., 1.1 th.; WA 13, fill above main room of Achaemenid Chapel, Level I, 7	Fig. 35:1
11 N 74	Head from baked-clay male(?) figurine wearing flat-topped hat; 2.5 h., 2.3 w.; WA 13, cut from Level I, 7	Fig. 35:2
11 N 75	Fragmentary rider wearing pointed helmet, from a baked-clay horse-and-rider figurine; 6.6 h., 3.1 w.; WA 13, cut from Level I, 7	Fig. 35:3
11 N 37	Pottery bowl; very fine, grit-tempered, cream ware, no slip; 7.0 h., 18.4 dm.; WA 12, Locus 1, Level I, 5	Fig. 35:4
11 N 46	Pottery jar with hole in base, used as part of drain; coarse, chaff-tempered greenish-buff ware, no slip; 36.0 h., 15.0 rim dm.; WA 12, Locus 1, Level I, 4	Fig. 35:5
11 N 79	Fragmentary baked-clay female figurine with hands clasped below breasts; 6.7 h., 3.1 w., 2.3 th.; WA 12, Locus 2, Floor 2	— —
11 N 92	Fragmentary pottery bowl; medium fine, chaff-tempered, buff ware, cream slip; 4.0 h., 10.7 dm.; WA 12, Locus 2, Floor 2	Fig. 35:6
11 N 93	Fragmentary pottery bowl; medium fine, chaff-tempered, buff ware, cream slip; 4.9 h., 10.8 dm.; WA 12, Locus 2, Floor 2	Fig. 35:7
11 N 96	Whole pottery bowl; medium fine, chaff-tempered, reddish ware, cream slip; 3.3 h., 9.6 dm.; WA 12, Locus 2, Floor 2	Fig. 35:8
11 N 82	Polished-bone spatula; broken; 11.1 l., 1.55 w.; WA 12, Locus 2, fill below Floor 1	— —
11 N 174	Bronze coin, badly worn; reverse destroyed; Seleucid, Antiochus IV (175–164 B.C.) or Demetrius I (162–150 B.C.); 1.55 dm., 0.35 th.; WA 12, Locus 2, fill below Floor 1	Fig. 36:1
11 N 69	Whole pottery bowl; medium fine, chaff-tempered, reddish ware, cream slip; 2.85 h., 9.45 dm.; WA 12, Locus 2, Floor 1	Fig. 36:2
11 N 70	Unbaked-clay triangular plumb bob or loom weight; 7.5 h., 3.2 × 3.1 base; WA 12, Locus 2, Floor 1	— —
11 N 83	Pottery jar with rounded bottom; medium fine, chaff-tempered, buff ware, cream slip; 10.7 h.,	Fig. 36:3

FIELD NUMBER	DESCRIPTION	ILLUSTRATION
	12.6 dm.; WA 12, Locus 2, Cache 1, cut down from Floor 1	
11 N 84	Pottery jar with rounded bottom; medium fine, chaff-tempered, buff ware, cream slip; 10.7 h., 13.0 dm.; WA 12, Locus 2, Cache 1, cut down from Floor 1	Fig. 36:4
11 N 85	Pottery jar with rounded bottom; medium fine, chaff-tempered, buff ware, cream slip; 9.9 h., 12.6 dm.; WA 12, Locus 2, Cache 2, cut down from Floor 1	Fig. 36:5
11 N 86	Pottery jar with rounded bottom; medium fine, chaff-tempered, buff ware, cream slip; 9.0 h., 13.0 dm.; WA 12, Locus 2, Cache 2, cut down from Floor 1	Fig. 36:6
11 N 87	Pottery jar with rounded bottom; medium fine, chaff-tempered, buff ware, cream slip; rim missing; 9.6 h., 14.5 dm.; WA 12, Locus 2, Cache 3, cut down from Floor 1	Fig. 36:7
11 N 88	Pottery jar with rounded bottom; medium fine, chaff-tempered, buff ware, cream slip; 12.1 h., 12.9 dm.; WA 12, Locus 2, Cache 4, cut down from Floor 0	Fig. 36:8
11 N 91	Baked brick with gaming board incised on it; 15.8 × 13.7 × 7.6; WA 12, Locus 2, Floor 0	Fig. 37:1
11 N 32	Brown stone bead; 0.9 dm.; WA 12, northwest of Locus 1, pit cut from Level I, 3	— —
11 N 38	Fragmentary miniature baked-clay bed with reed mat webbing indicated; see *Nippur* I, Pl. 144:3, 4; 6.75 l., 6.4 w.; WA 12, northeast of Locus 1, Level I, 3	— —
11 N 89	Fragment of hollow figurine; subject unrecognizable; 4.8 h., 4.3 w., 0.7 th.; WA 12, northwest of Locus 1, Level I, 2	Fig. 37:2
11 N 90	Fragmentary hollow horse-and-rider figurine; Hellenistic style; 5.7 h., 4.1 w., 0.7 th.; WA 12, northwest of Locus 1, Level I, 2	Fig. 37:3
11 N 17	Fragmentary baked-clay plaque; hindquarters of male lion; 6.2 h., 5.6 w.; WA 12, northwest of Locus 1, Level I, 1	Fig. 37:4
11 N 19	Whole pottery bowl; medium fine, chaff-tempered, reddish ware, cream slip; 4.4–4.8 h., 10.9–11.1 dm.; WA 12, northwest of Locus 1, Level I, 1	— —
11 N 80	Fragment of rider with cap curling over to front, from horse-and-rider figurine; 5.55 h., 4.1 w.; WA 12, north of Locus 1, Level I; floor not determined	— —

FIELD NUMBER	DESCRIPTION	ILLUSTRATION
11 N 81	Polished kidney-shaped agate bead; 3.2 l., 1.85 w., 0.65 th.; see *Persepolis* II, Pl. 44:11—13; WA 12, north of Locus 1, Level I; floor not determined	Fig. 37:5
11 N 66	Fragmentary baked-clay nude female figurine; 6.4 h., 4.1 w., 2.9 th.; WA 12, northwest of Locus 1, Level I; floor not determined	——

Intrusive in upper levels or from surface debris

11 N 33	Fragment of baked-clay plaque; legs of male figure with pedestal on one side and animal skin(?) on the other; Herakles(?); 6.9 h., 8.0 w., 3.2 th.; see *Nippur* I, Pl. 139:4; WA 12, in Parthian drain cutting east corner of Locus 1	Fig. 37:6
11 N 7	Rim sherd of incantation bowl with two lines of Mandaic script; medium coarse, chaff-tempered, yellowish ware, reddish slip; 4.1 h., 6.5 w., 0.54 th.; see Appendix C for discussion; WA, sand above Level I	Fig. 38:1
11 N 8	Potsherd with incantation in Jewish script on both sides; fine, chaff-tempered greenish ware, no slip; 6.0 h., 6.0 w., 0.8 th.; see Appendix C for discussion; WA, sand above Level I	Fig. 38:2
11 N 9	Rim sherd of incantation bowl with four lines of script; medium coarse, chaff-tempered, buff ware, greenish slip; 6.6 h., 19.3 w., 12.4 dm. originally; WA, sand above Level I	Fig. 38:3
11 N 10	Baked-clay, hollow bird figurine, whole; traces of red paint on beak, wing edges, tail; 9.5 h., 11.5 l., 5.3 w.; WA 24, cut made for railroad	——
11 N 11	Pottery jar, fine cream ware, with interior and exterior white glaze; Parthian; 6.0 h., 7.0 dm.; from a slipper coffin found during laying of railroad in WA 24	——
11 N 12	Unglazed pottery jar; rim missing; medium fine, grit-tempered, greenish ware, cream slip; 4.6 h., 5.0 dm.; same locus as 11 N 11, above	——
11 N 13	Fragmentary baked-clay female figurine; Parthian style; 6.2 h., 4.4 w., 3.0 th.; see Legrain, *Terra-Cottas from Nippur* (Philadelphia, 1930) Nos. 110, 136; WA, surface	——
11 N 94	Baked-clay horse figurine; 5.1 h., 2.0 w., 7.4 l.; WA 12, inside mud brick of Wall B	——
11 N 116	Badly worn shell cylinder seal; Akkadian; 3.15 h., 1.9 dm.; WA 24, in cut made to lay railroad	Fig. 38:5
11 N 196	Bronze coin; Parthian, king facing left with hair in knot and pointed beard, wearing helmet, on obverse; Tyche facing left, on reverse; WA 24, surface debris	——

Objects from WA 7, 8, northwest of Wall C

The objects from these squares cannot be located precisely. Most came from ancient fill associated with the foundations of Walls AD and C. It was often difficult to distinguish one layer of fill from another.

Deep in fill near or within walls (probably the same as Level IV of WA 12, 13)

FIELD NUMBER	DESCRIPTION	ILLUSTRATION
11 N 163	Flat, round glazed frit bead with raised decoration of circles and dots; 2.85–3.05 dm., 0.6 th.; WA 8, fill within Walls AL—AN	——
11 N 164	Polished-bone spatula; 10.9 l., 1.9 w.; same locus as 11 N 163	——
11 N 168	Stone pestle with peck marks on ends; 11.55 l., 2.9 w.; same locus as 11 N 163	——
11 N 169	Polished-bone spatula; 17.5 l., 2.8 w.; same locus as 11 N 163	——
11 N 14	Fragmentary rider with cap pointing forward, from horse-and-rider figurine; 6.0 h., 2.0 w.; WA 7, fill for Wall C or later	——
11 N 21	Rim sherd of incantation bowl with three lines of Jewish script; see Appendix C for discussion; 4.5 h., 4.9 w.; WA 7, fill; Pennsylvania cut(?)	Fig. 38:4
11 N 34	Trilobate copper arrowhead; 4.05 l., 1.25 w.; WA 7, fill for Wall C	——
11 N 40	Fragmentary animal figurine, probably horse, with rein lines across nose; 7.9 h., 3.7 w.; WA 7, fill	——
11 N 43	Fragmentary rider with peaked cap, from horse-and-rider figurine; 6.7 h., 4.05 w.; WA 8, fill for Wall C or later	——
11 N 44	Fragmentary baked-clay figurine of a tambourine player with double-strand necklace; 5.4 h., 7.2 w., 2.1 th.; see Fig. 74:1 for same type; WA 8, fill for Wall C or later	——
11 N 35	Polished-bone hairpin with incised lines on end; 16.4 l., 0.55 dm.; WA 8, fill above Wall C	——
11 N 36	Fragmentary rider with high cap bent to front, from baked-clay horse-and-rider figurine; 7.1 h., 4.0 w.; WA 8, fill above Wall C	——

1

2

3a 3b

Fig. 28.—Objects from Old Babylonian levels in pit sunk below Neo-Babylonian Temple Rooms 1 and 2

1

2

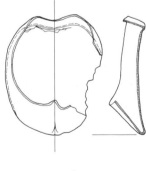

3

4

Fig. 29.—Objects from Old Babylonian levels in pit sunk below Neo-Babylonian Temple Rooms 1 and 2 (1, 2) and from the Neo-Babylonian level (3, 4)

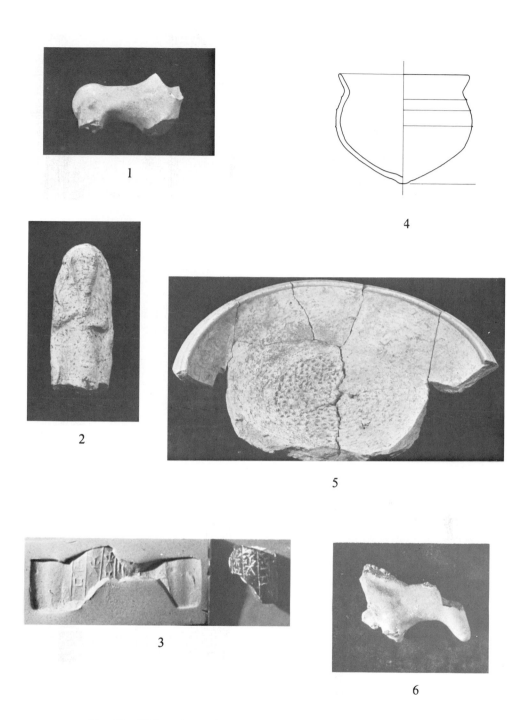

Fig. 30.—Objects from the area enclosed by Wall P in WA 8–13

1

2

3a

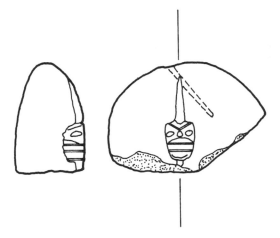

3b

Fig. 31.—Objects from above Wall P in WA 8—13

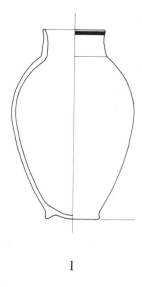

1

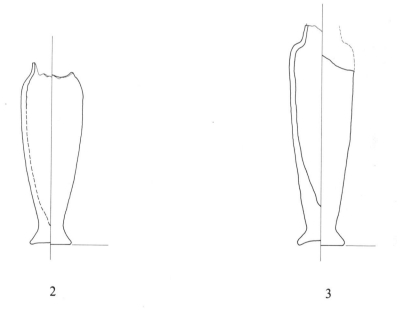

2   3

Fig. 32.—Pottery from WA, levels V (1) and IV (2, 3)

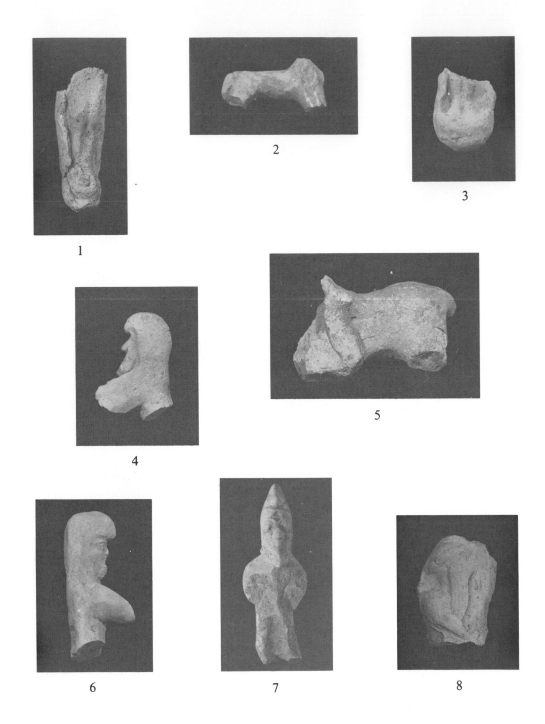

Fig. 33.—Figurines from various levels in WA

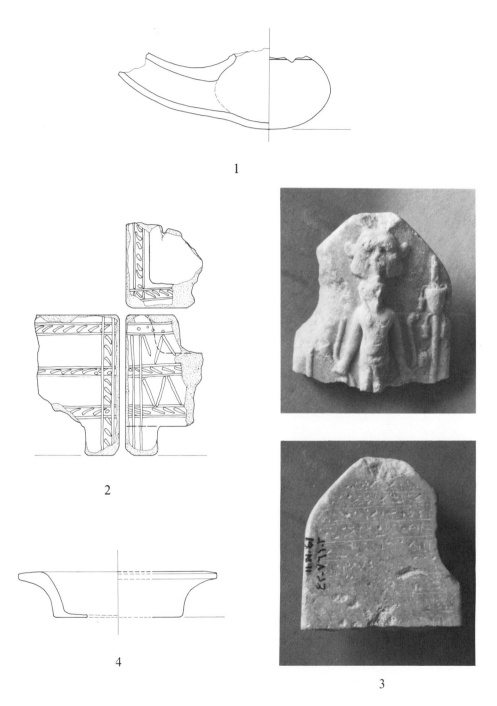

1

2

4

3

Fig. 34.—Pottery from WA Level III (1, 2) and a stone *cippus* (3) and vessel (4) from the Achaemenid Chapel in Level II.

51

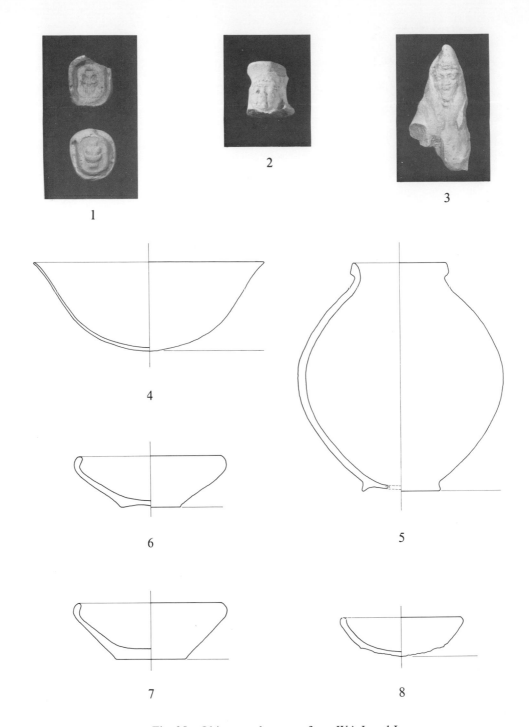

1

2

3

4

6

5

7

8

Fig. 35.—Objects and pottery from WA Level I

52

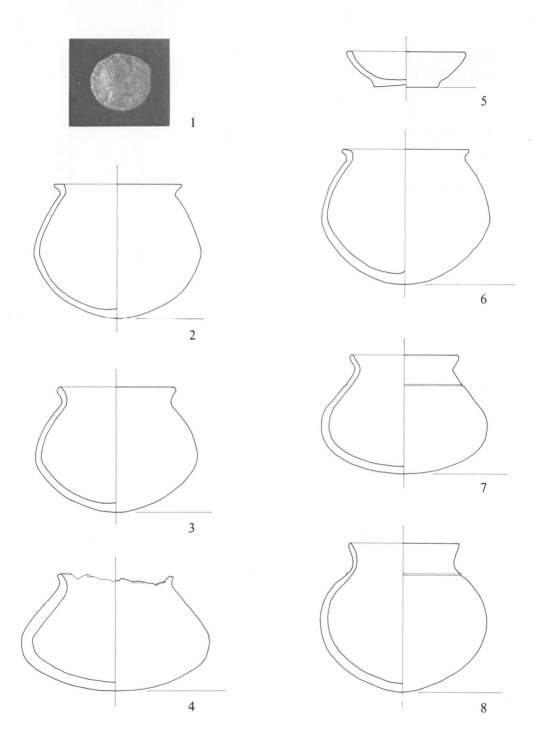

Fig. 36.—A coin and pottery caches from WA 12, Locus 1, Level I, Seleucid

Fig. 37.—Objects from WA 12, Level I; No. 6 is intrusive in a drain

1

2 *a*

2 *b*

3

4

5

Fig. 38.—Aramaic bowl fragments (1–4) and a worn Akkadian shell seal found in late context (5).

NIPPUR CERAMIC CODE*

Explanation of the number code accompanying each sherd:

Digit Characteristic

1	Color of sherd
2	Consistency of paste
3	Temper
4	Surface treatment
5	Color of surface
6	Decoration on sherd

In particular, the numbers of the code mean:

Number	1st Digit	2d Digit	3d Digit	4th Digit	5th Digit	6th Digit
0	Buff	Very fine	Chaff	None	Yellowish	Incised, straight line
1	Cream	Fine	Grit	Slip	Reddish	Incised, wavy line
2	Yellowish	Medium fine	Shell	Burnish	Cream	Ribbing
3	Greenish	Medium coarse		Glaze	Greenish	Painted figure
4	Reddish	Coarse			Bluish	Painted motif
5	Orange	Very coarse			Red	Stamped
6	Gray	Extremely coarse			Plum Red	Other
7	Grayish					
8	Black					
9	Green (overfired)					

*Adapted from R. McC. Adams and H. J. Nissen, *The Uruk Countryside* (Chicago, 1972) p. 107.

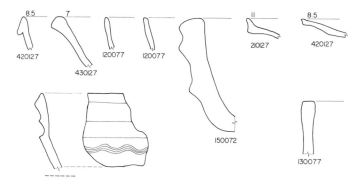

WA 12 TEMPLE ROOM 2 FL.12

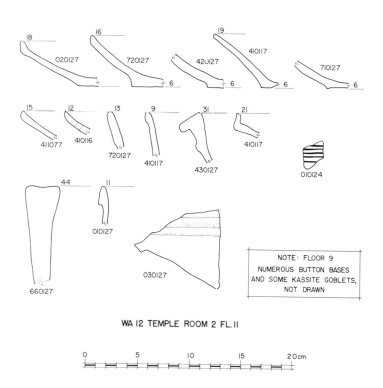

NOTE: FLOOR 9
NUMEROUS BUTTON BASES
AND SOME KASSITE GOBLETS,
NOT DRAWN

WA 12 TEMPLE ROOM 2 FL.11

Fig. 39.—Sherds from Temple Room 2, Old Babylonian floors

Note: Numbers at rims and some bases indicate diameters in centimeters where possible to calculate.

57

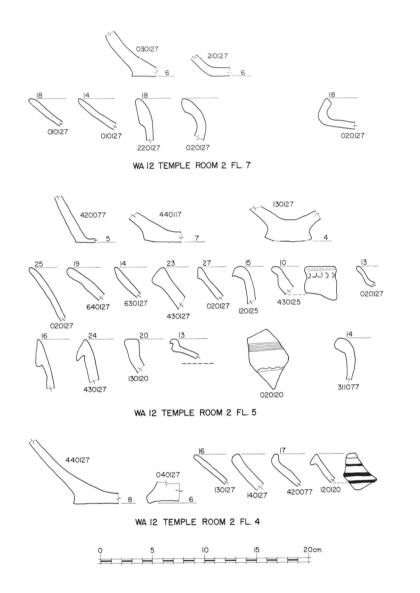

WA 12 TEMPLE ROOM 2 FL. 7

WA 12 TEMPLE ROOM 2 FL. 5

WA 12 TEMPLE ROOM 2 FL. 4

Fig. 40.—Sherds from Temple Room 2, Middle Babylonian and Neo-Babylonian floors.

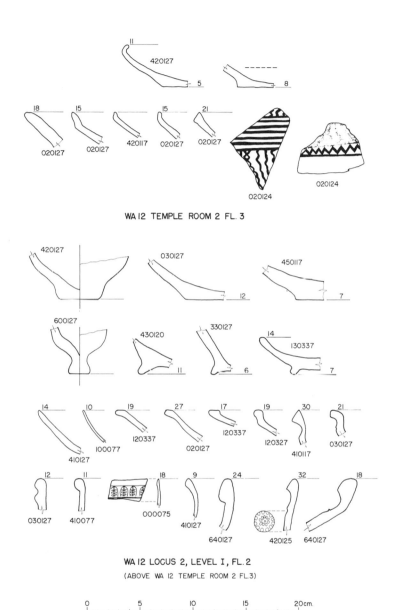

WA 12 TEMPLE ROOM 2 FL. 3

WA 12 LOCUS 2, LEVEL I, FL. 2

(ABOVE WA 12 TEMPLE ROOM 2 FL.3)

0   5   10   15   20cm.

Fig. 41.—Sherds from Temple Room 2, Neo-Babylonian, and from Locus 2, above it, Achaemenid.

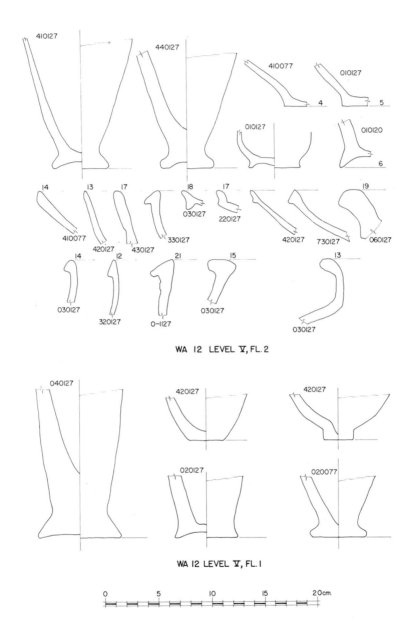

WA 12 LEVEL V, FL. 2

WA 12 LEVEL V, FL. 1

Fig. 42.—Sherds from Old Babylonian floors outside temple

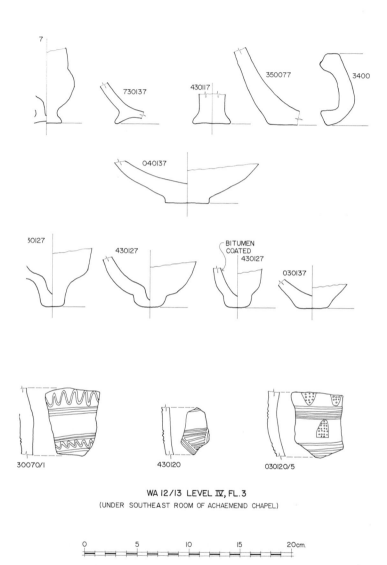

7

730137

430117   350077   3400

040137

30127   430127   BITUMEN COATED 430127   030137

30070/1   430120   030120/5

WA 12/13 LEVEL IV, FL.3
(UNDER SOUTHEAST ROOM OF ACHAEMENID CHAPEL)

0   5   10   15   20cm.

Fig. 43.—Sherds from Kassite floor outside temple

61

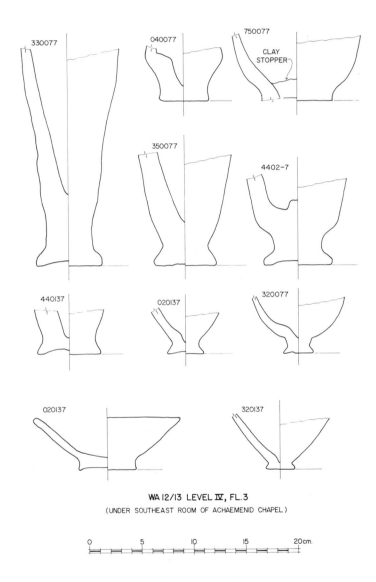

330077

040077

750077
CLAY
STOPPER

350077

4402-7

440137

020137

320077

020137

320137

WA 12/13 LEVEL IV, FL.3
(UNDER SOUTHEAST ROOM OF ACHAEMENID CHAPEL)

0   5   10   15   20cm.

Fig. 44.—Sherds from Kassite floor outside temple

62

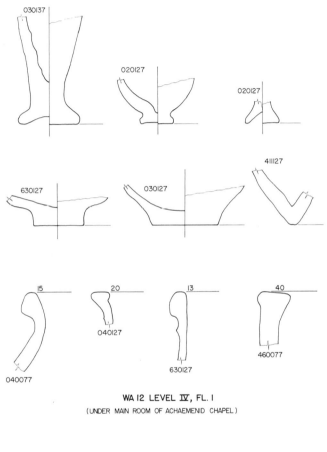

030137

020127

020127

411127

630127

030127

15

20

13

40

040127

040077

630127

460077

WA 12 LEVEL IV, FL. I
(UNDER MAIN ROOM OF ACHAEMENID CHAPEL)

0   5   10   15   20cm.

Fig. 45.—Sherds from late Kassite or Middle Babylonian floor outside temple.

63

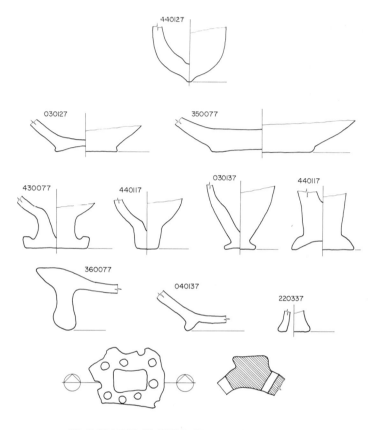

WA 12/13 LEVEL IV, INSIDE AREA ENCLOSED BY P WALLS

Fig. 46.—Sherds from Kassite or Middle Babylonian floors associated with Wall P

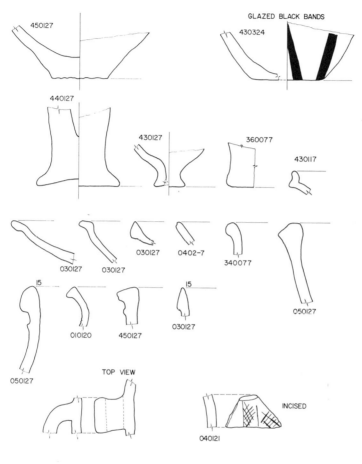

GLAZED BLACK BANDS

450127

430324

440127

430127

360077

430117

030127   0402-7

340077

030127   030127

15

15

010120   450127

030127

050127

050127

TOP VIEW

INCISED

040121

WA 12/13 LEVEL III, FL. 4

(UNDER SOUTHEAST ROOM OF ACHAEMENID CHAPEL)

0   5   10   15   20cm.

Fig. 47.—Sherds from Neo-Babylonian floor outside temple

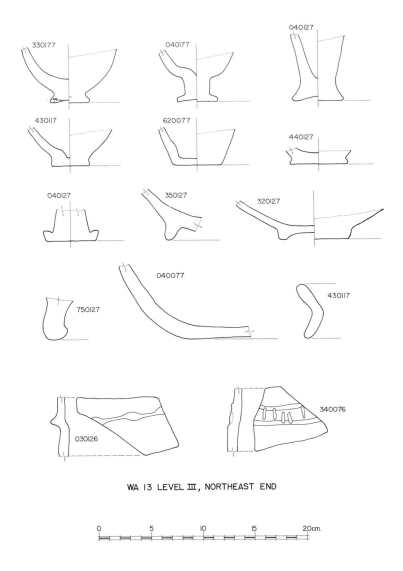

WA 13 LEVEL III, NORTHEAST END

Fig. 48.—Sherds from Neo-Babylonian floors outside temple

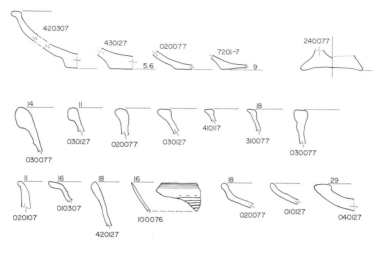

WA 12 LEVEL II, FL. 2

(UNDER MAIN ROOM OF ACHAEMENID CHAPEL)

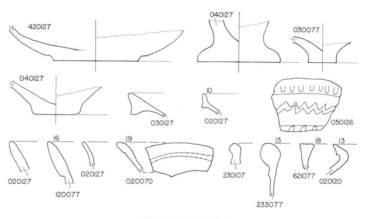

WA 12 LEVEL II, FL. 2

(UNDER SOUTHEAST ROOM OF ACHAEMENID CHAPEL)

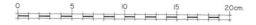

0   5   10   15   20cm.

Fig. 49.—Sherds from Achaemenid floor under Chapel

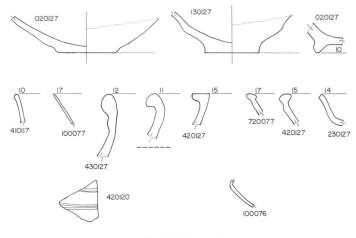

WA 12 LEVEL II, FL. I
(MAIN ROOM OF ACHAEMENID CHAPEL)

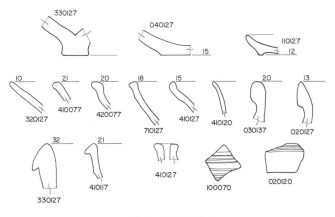

WA 12 LEVEL II, FL. I
(SOUTHEAST ROOM OF ACHAEMENID CHAPEL)

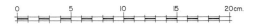

Fig. 50.—Sherds from the Achaemenid Chapel

WA 12 NORTHWEST OF LOCUS I, LEVEL I, FL. 4

Fig. 51.—Sherds from Seleucid floor above chapel

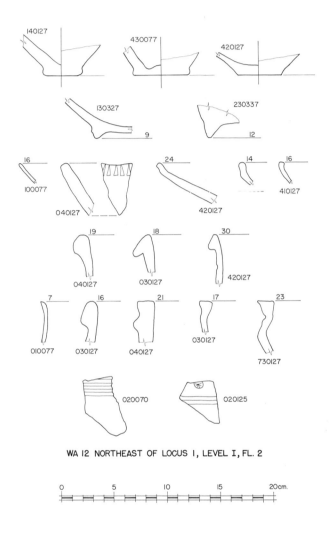

WA 12 NORTHEAST OF LOCUS I, LEVEL I, FL. 2

0   5   10   15   20cm.

Fig. 52.—Sherds from Seleucid floor above chapel

III

AREA WA 50c

In the beginning of the season, while most of the labor force was engaged in laying track, setting up the railroad, and removing sand from WA, we began a 5 × 5 m. stratigraphic pit in a gully south of the main work (Fig. 53A, B). This pit, located at a point more than a meter below the level of the Court of Columns, would, we thought, allow us to find out quickly what strata lay below and would indicate how far down Kassite levels were. Initially thought of as a short-term operation, the pit proved so interesting and yielded such useful information that it was carried on almost to the end of the season. Work was stopped at a depth of 8 m., where it became too dangerous. There were several major levels to be distinguished in the pit (Fig. 54). The earliest was related to a set of walls of unbaked plano-convex bricks (Fig. 56A) constructed in several phases (Fig. 55). Wall A originated at some point lower than our excavation and was not constructed of solid mud brick but was actually a mud wall incorporating intermittent courses of plano-convex bricks (Fig. 56B). Mr. Haines said that he had encountered a similar construction, with the outer faces of walls done in brick and filled in with mud, in the North Temple at Nippur. Wall B, which was cut into and joined Wall A, was definitely a later construction, resting on Level X, 7, which was a reed-mat layer. Wall D, in the southeast profile (Figs. 56A, 57), seems to have been built at the same time as Wall B, since it also sits on Level X, 7. However, the plano-convex mud bricks used in Walls B and D were different colors. In Wall B, the bricks were brown, like those in Wall A, whereas in Wall D, the bricks were black. Wall C, a somewhat later addition, also had black mud bricks. There was also a variation in the size of the bricks. Wall A had 33 × 15 × 7.5 cm. bricks, Wall B had 22 × 15 × 5 cm., whereas Wall C had 26 × 15 × 4.5 cm.

Wall D had plaster on both its northwest and northeast faces. Not much of the northeast face was exposed in our cut but enough investigation was done to establish the plastering. Wall C, initially built without a doorway to divide the space between Walls B and D, rested on Level X, 7.

The first proper occupation floor in the building was Level X, 6, a well laid plaster that also ran up the walls. In the "court" to the southwest of

71

Wall C, a bitumen-lined basin was found resting on Level X, 5. It was about 30 cm. in height and went out of use before Level X, 4, which ran over it. Northwest, across Wall B, were two clay bread ovens. These continued in use into Level X, 3. As the floor rose around the ovens, bread-makers would have had to reach down inside to attach the flat cakes to the inside. Similar sub-surface ovens are used today in the Nippur area, as are examples rising above ground level.

Level X, 3 was another plaster floor that ran up from Room 1 through a newly cut doorway into the "court." A storage jar, sunk to its neck in the court, and a white stone mortar must have had some functional relationship (Fig. 57). Samples were taken from the jar and the mortar for analysis.

At the same time the doorway was being cut through Wall C, Wall A underwent a renovation. From Level X, 3 upward the mud bricks were much better laid (Fig. 56*B*). Wall B seems not to have needed restoration (Fig. 56*A*).

Above a well preserved Floor 2, with a basin in Area 1, and a damaged Floor 1, the walls seem to have been leveled for a rebuilding on the stubs. Level IX (Figs. 54, 57) saw a continuation in the use of plano-convex mud bricks.

Levels X and IX, since plano-convex mud bricks were employed there, would traditionally be assigned a date in the Early Dynastic Period. Only a few sherds, however, and perhaps one jar (11 N 192, Fig. 67:2) from Level X, 7 would allow such a dating. From at least Level X, 6 the material was Akkadian.[1] Especially definitive was a cylinder seal showing gods in conflict (11 N 130, Fig. 68:2). This seal was found in the court on Floor 4 along with three miniature pottery vessels (11 N 121—23, Fig. 67:5—7) and a stone cosmetic tray (11 N 131, Fig. 68:3). Even more important, in Room 1 on the same floor were four Old Akkadian tablets dealing with distribution of baskets, sheep, and metals (Appendix A, Nos. 1—4).

Level X, Floor 3 also yielded a cylinder seal of Early Dynastic style (11 N 139, Fig. 68:9), clearly a holdover. In the north corner of the court, at Level X, 3 was a group of vessels, probably functionally related. A stone cup (11 N 112, Fig. 68:4) lay near a group of pottery bowls. One bowl (11 N 119) rested on the floor with another (11 N 118, Fig. 68:6) nesting inside. Upside down over them was a third bowl (11 N 120). A slightly different type of bowl (11 N 117, Fig. 68:5) lay on its side nearby.

Floor 2, the last well preserved floor in Level X, also gave good dating evidence in the form of a broken Ekur brick stamp of Naram-Sin (Appendix A, No. 36, Fig. 69:3) from Area 1, northeast of Room 1, and a cylinder seal fragment of clearly late Akkadian style (11 N 126, Fig. 68:7), the latter from

---

1. In my "Umm el-Jīr, a Town in Akkad," *JNES* XXXI (1972) 237—94, on much weaker evidence, I suggested that plano-convex bricks were used well into the Akkadian Period. Our findings in WA 50*c* confirm that suggestion with certainty. At Umm el-Jīr, ribbed sherds and some black-painted ribbed ware occurred, along with comb-incised and a few examples of fine gray ware. It may be that at Umm el-Jīr this material was also post-Akkadian.

the courtyard. Found in the same locus as the brick stamp but closer to a baked-clay basin was a small jar (11 N 110, Fig. 69:1) containing a hoard of copper objects (11 N 111, Fig. 69:2).

The destruction and rebuilding that resulted in Level IX seem to have been done around the end of the Akkadian Period. A cylinder seal (11 N 97, Fig. 70:1) from Floor IXc is Akkadian in motif but degenerate in style. The sherds in this level carry on types from Level X but show somewhat more ribbing, and there is a beginning of applied decoration.

Immediately above Level IX was a thick stratum of burned and ashy debris. This level, VIII, was relatively featureless except for a bit of mud-brick wall, one course high, in the northern corner of the pit (Fig. 58). The mud bricks of this wall measured 30 × 15 × 8.5–11.0 cm. The size of these bricks and the sherds from Level VIII were very similar to some I had called Akkadian at Umm el-Jīr.[2]

At Level VII, there was a definite break. The small wall in the south corner, composed of mud bricks measuring 14 × ? × 6.5 cm., was associated with a group of sherds very different from those of the previous level. There were, in fact, almost no rim profiles shared with Level VIII, but some that would be classed as Ur III or even Isin-Larsa. Within this level, against the southeastern profile, there was a clay oven (Fig. 59) whose structure could not be worked out precisely. To the northwest was a round hearth, ringed with baked bricks. Nearby was a grave that had been cut in from above. The bricks of the hearth and the grave lay just below and were covered by Level VIe, a sand lens about 2 cm. thick. The burial was of a small child. Over the head had been placed an overturned bowl (11 N 60, Fig. 70:8) and near the face were two jars (11 N 58, 59, Figs. 70:6–7). The pottery seems best dated to the Kassite Period. This was the only Kassite material found in WA 50c, because just above Level VIe, the floors were, at the earliest, Neo-Babylonian in time. In three centimeters, we made a jump of more than a thousand years. It is clear that the builders of the wall in Level VI (Figs. 54, 60, 61) had first excavated and removed whatever occupation layers had been above Level VII, had cut a shallow trench and put in their foundation walls, then had strewn clean sand in the open court that our excavation partly exposed. There were three fairly thick plasterings of the wall, all running down to the sand lens. An earlier plastering that ran a few centimeters below the sand (Fig. 54) must have been the initial plaster applied when the wall was first built. The fact that the sand abutted this earliest plaster shows that it was deliberately laid after the construction of the wall.

The wall in Level VI was taken apart course by course to examine its construction. The foundation course (Fig. 60) was mud brick, but the doorway was outlined in fragments of baked bricks. The door socket on the inside of the building was also baked brick and was edged with upright baked bricks to form a box below floor level. The courses of mud brick were

2. *Ibid.*, pp. 253 ff.

laid in irregular alternations of sizes, 30 × 30 × 10 cm. and 30 × 15 × 10 cm. Sometimes the half-sizes were laid on edge (as in Fig. 61, which shows Level VI*d*). At this point, a proper, plastered floor was found inside the building, running to a baked-brick doorsill. Later renovations (e.g., Level VI*c*) carried the plaster over the sill.

At Level VI *d*, the courtyard was furnished with a curving horizontal drain or runnel of baked brick that sloped toward the northeast. Alongside this runnel was a drain that was carried down through the lowest levels we excavated.

A round pit in the southeastern end originated sometime later than Level VI*d* but before VI*c* (Fig. 61). This pit, which had thin layers of ash, was perhaps a cooking facility of some sort. From the debris within the pit came firm dating evidence in the form of a late Babylonian contract (Appendix A, No. 26) dated to the reign of Cyrus II (538–530 B.C.). The document concerns the renting of a boat by a man named Ninurta-erîba to Šamaš-aḫa-iddin, Tattanu, and Sîn-zēr-ibnī. On the edge of the tablet is inscribed in Aramaic "belonging to Tattanu," as Dr. Kaufman shows in Appendix C. In the pit was also a clay tablet fragment inscribed only in Aramaic (11 NT 8, Appendix C). Given the dated tablet and the situation of the pit, we can state that most of the floors associated with the wall were of Achaemenid date. The building, of which it is a part, may have been constructed in late Neo-Babylonian times, but it was used mainly under the Persians.

Within Level VI there were found two burials, one with a bathtub-like pottery coffin (Fig. 62). Both burials may have been cut from high up in Level VI, but the upper part of this stratum was badly destroyed by pits and the origin for the graves was not discernible. They probably were cut from Level V. The date for the burials is Achaemenid or Seleucid. Burial 1, resting on or about Level VI*b*, had no coffin. The skeleton, a woman of more than middle age, lay flexed on the right side and was oriented with the head to the southeast. Found with the skeleton were three glazed jars, an unglazed bowl, a copper bowl, a copper reticule, a copper finger ring, a bone spatula, a bone hairpin, and a bead necklace (11 N 22–31, Fig. 72:1–9).

Burial 2, in a pottery coffin (Fig. 63), had similar material (Fig. 73:1–7). The skeleton lay on its right side, flexed, with its head to the southeast. In front of the body, at the waist, there were two green glazed jars (11 N 47, 48), a copper pin (11 N 50), and a bone spatula (11 N 51). Around the left arm were frit beads (11 N 52). A bone spatula was near the hands (11 N 51), and a bronze pendant of a *puzuzu* demon (11 N 53) found under the pelvis may have been originally tied to a cord around the waist.

After the destruction of the wall in Level VI, the area was used as a refuse dump. The section we show (Fig. 54) does not give an indication of the ancient slope and the layers of debris that pitched sharply toward the north. A photograph of the southwest profile makes the situation clear (Fig. 64*A*). There were pits, filled with ash and other material, that were certainly cut from within Level VI. It was almost impossible, however, to distinguish be-

tween cuts made from this level and the next higher one, V. In one such cut
was found a Late Babylonian letter with its envelope (Appendix A, No. 27).

On the northeastern side of the square, in a rough pit lying within Level
VI, but probably originating from Level V, were found two whole tablets
and one fragment (11 NT 3—5), which are medical commentaries of a man
named Enlil-Kaşir. Miguel Civil discusses these Seleucid texts in Appendix
A of this report and will publish them fully elsewhere. Another fragment of
uncertain content (Appendix A, No. 32) was found in the same context.

The sherds from Level VI showed a marked change from those below.
Previously, there had been no eggshell, no black wares, and no glazed wares.
In Level VI, out of a total of 6,818 sherds, 301 were glazed and 401 were
eggshell. In Level VII, there were only a few fragments of equid figurines,
but in Level VI there were 26, most of them being of the horse-and-rider
type (e.g., Fig. 71:2). There were also a fragmentary figurine of a monkey
(11 N 20, Fig. 71:3) and a baked clay bulla with a round impression of a
lion walking to the right (11 N 55, Fig. 71:5).

There was in the fill above Level VIa a very unusual jar with lug handles
(11 N 193). This vessel (Fig. 71:6) had crudely incised linear decoration on
the body, wavy incisions and punctations on the neck. The neck and rim
profile is familiar among Neo-Babylonian, Achaemenid, and later jars, but
the treatment of the surface is not. In general, the vessel seems to be a precursor of Parthian storage jars. Probably it is to be dated Seleucid.

Level V was a very difficult stratum to excavate. The bits of mud-brick
wall visible in the eastern and southern corners of the square (Fig. 54) are
misleading. We were unable to find faces or trace these walls. Their
construction was haphazard. The entire area continued to be used for dumping trash, and the walls must have been insubstantial, short-term construc-
tions. In this level, we found 7,812 sherds, the largest number from any level.
The sherds were mainly of the same basic shapes and decoration as those
from Level VI. In terms of percentages, there was as much use of eggshell
and glazed wares but a sharp drop in fine black wares

Among other things found in this area at Level V was the skeleton of an
ass (Fig. 64B). The bones were collected for full analysis.

With Level IV, the area took on a more occupational character again. The
decrease in the number of sherds (4,759) reflects this shift. In terms of percentages, there was a drop in eggshell and black wares but about the same
proportion of glazed sherds.

Level III is evidenced only by some tamped earth and ash-strewn floors.
The floors of Levels III and IV were cut to put in the foundations of a building whose north corner we touched. The section (Fig. 54) is slightly misleading, in that the ash-filled cut beside the wall might be interpreted as the
foundation trench and would then necessitate the assigning of this wall to
Level I. This cut, however, was definitely not associated with the foundation
for the building and, in fact, destroyed the evidence for that construction
operation at the point where our excavation met the baulk. Level II (Fig. 65)

must be seen as the main stratum associated with the building. A line just under Level II, marked "salt line" on the section, seems to be the remains of a reed-mat layer laid down while the building was being constructed.

The sherds from Level III and Level II seem, on cursory examination, to be similar in types, decoration, and material to those from Level IV. Glazed sherds and eggshell and black wares all occurred. At Level II, however, there was a distinct increase in the use of stamps for decorating unglazed vessels. (Stamps appeared first in Level VI and continued through Level I.) The types of stamps, the shapes on which they are found, and the distinction by levels have not yet been worked out but will, I think, play a great part in distinguishing Achaemenid from Seleucid material.

There was a difference in glazes between Levels VI–III and II. From Levels VI through III, glaze had almost always been light green in color. At Level II, however, green glaze was relatively rare, while a white glaze was the most common color. In this level there was also an introduction of yellow glaze. One could argue that the white glaze might have been originally light green, which, because of some chemical reaction, had turned white. But the introduction of the yellow must be seen as definitely marking a break. It should be pointed out, however, that glazed sherds even in Level II did not make up much of the total (87 out of 2,108 sherds).

Level I, preserved in only part of the square and represented by a small wall set atop the more massive wall of Level II, had along the southeastern baulk a baked-brick basin originally lined with bitumen (Figs. 65, 66). A drain led out of the northwest side. Nearby was a round clay oven.

Level I was badly cut by later people and erosion and was overlaid by sand and clay wash. From the untouched floors sherds were collected. Shapes and decoration seemed to continue from Level II. A few dark green glazed sherds may have been intrusive from Parthian levels not preserved above.

In summary, WA 50c may be said to have supplied a sample of sherds from two crucial ranges of time. From below Level VIe, we have material for distinguishing Akkadian from Ur III/Isin-Larsa pottery. We may even be able to show significant changes within the Akkadian Period.

Above Level VIe, we have what may be a crucial sample for the Neo-Babylonian through Seleucid range of pottery. Such material is not yet well enough known, and it is my opinion that much of what has previously been called Neo-Babylonian is actually Achaemenid, and part of what has been called Achaemenid is actually Seleucid. The bulk of sherds from this operation was so great (over 40,000 sherds) that, even though body sherds were discarded, analysis could not be completed in time for this report. This work will be done and the results will appear in the final monograph.

A

B

Fig. 53.—Photograph showing relationship of main area of WA to WA 50c, which is in the background to the southeast (*A*) and in (*B*), from east, in foreground.

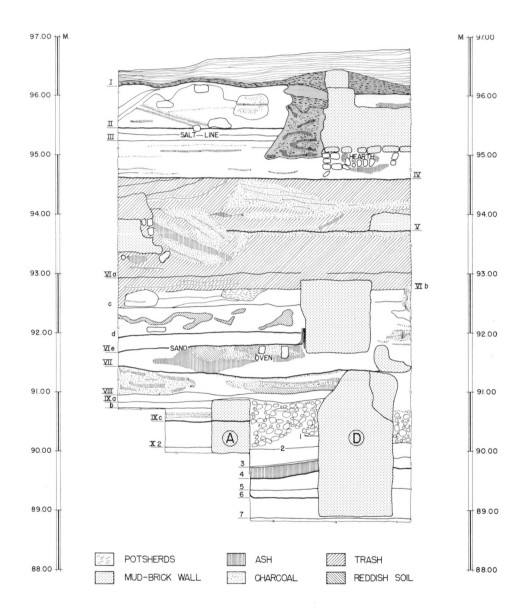

Fig. 54.—Section of southeast profile of WA 50*c*

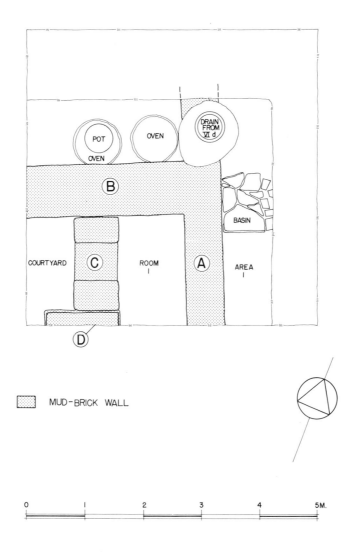

Fig. 55.—Plan of WA 50c, Level X. Ovens rest on Floor 6, basin in Area 1 rests on Floor 2.

A

B

Fig. 56.—*A*. Area WA 50*c*, Level X, from the east. Doorway in Wall C at
Floor 3, with renovation of the wall at that level. To the right, Wall B is
one construction with no renovation. *B*. Area WA 50*c*, Level X, Wall A, from
the west, showing construction in mud with occasional mud bricks. Better
laid courses are above Floor 3.

Fig. 57.—Area WA 50c, Level X, Floor 3, from the northwest. In the background is the courtyard, with a storage jar sunk into the floor and a mortar beside it.

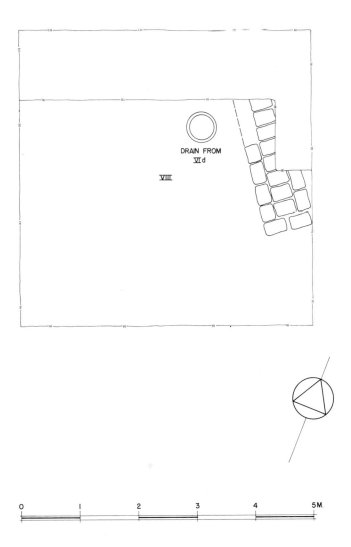

DRAIN FROM
VI d

VIII

0   1   2   3   4   5M.

Fig. 58.—Plan of WA 50c, Level VIII

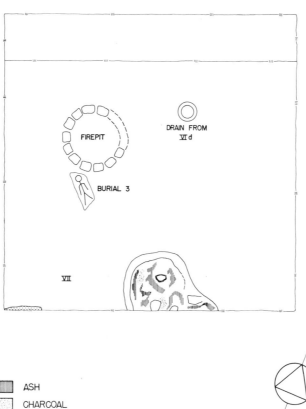

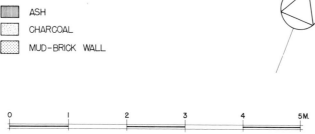

ASH

CHARCOAL

MUD-BRICK WALL

Fig. 59.—Plan of WA 50c, Level VII

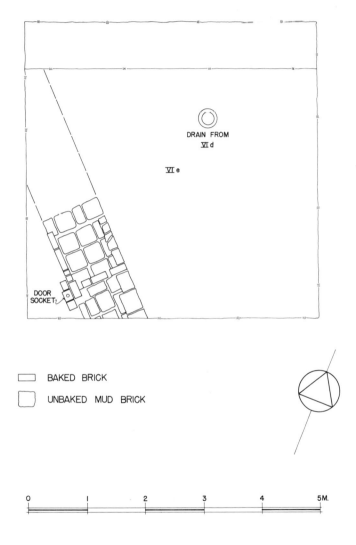

DRAIN FROM
VI d

VI e

DOOR
SOCKET?

▢ BAKED BRICK

▢ UNBAKED MUD BRICK

0   1   2   3   4   5M.

Fig. 60.—Plan of WA 50c, Level VIe, showing the foundation
course of the wall.

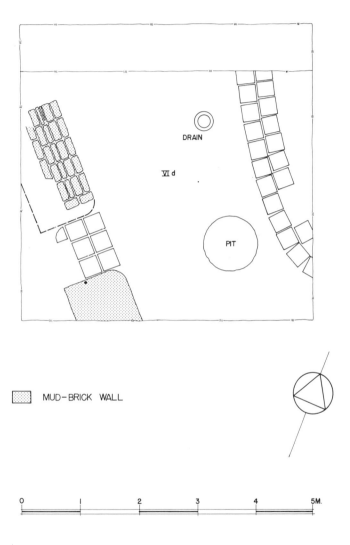

DRAIN

ⅥI d

PIT

MUD-BRICK WALL

0   1   2   3   4   5M.

Fig. 61.—Plan of WA 50c, Level VIc, with upper part of the wall and drain

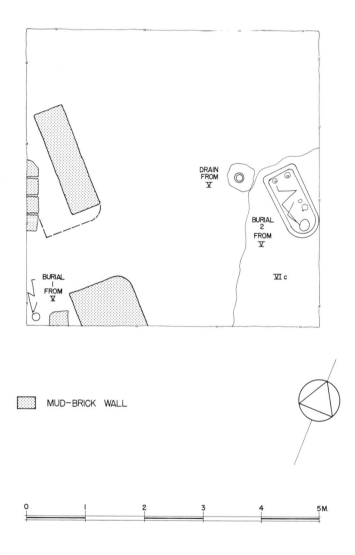

DRAIN
FROM
V

BURIAL
2
FROM
V

VIc

BURIAL
1
FROM
V

MUD–BRICK WALL

0   1   2   3   4   5M.

Fig. 62.–Plan of WA 50c, Level VIc, with burials intrusive from Level V

Fig. 63.—Burial 2 in Area WA 50c, Level V, from above

A

B

Fig. 64.—*A*. General view of Area WA 50*c*, from the north showing upper levels with trash pits visible as light areas on baulks. *B*. Equid skeleton in WA 50*c*, Level V, from the northwest.

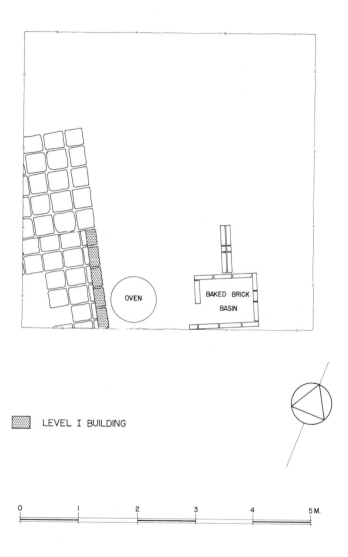

OVEN

BAKED BRICK
BASIN

LEVEL I BUILDING

0   1   2   3   4   5 M.

Fig. 65.—Plan of WA 50c, Levels II and I

89

Fig. 66.—Basin and oven in WA 50c, Level I, from the south

CATALOGUE OF OBJECTS
BY LOCUS AND LEVEL IN WA 50*c*

FIELD NUMBER	DESCRIPTION*	ILLUSTRATION
Level X		
11 N 175	Pottery jar; medium fine, chaff-tempered, grayish buff ware, cream slip; 6.8 h., dm. 7.15; below Floor 7	Fig. 67:1
11 N 192	High-necked pottery jar; medium fine, chaff-tempered, buff ware, cream slip, spout missing, 28.2 h., 14.0 dm.; see *Nippur* I, Pl. 80:14; Floor 7	Fig. 67:2
11 N 138	Crude, handmade miniature pottery bowl with three feet; 3.2–3.9 h., 4.7–5.0 dm.; see *Nippur* I, Pl. 80:3, 4;.Level X, Floor 6, Room 1	Fig. 67:3
11 N 140	Miniature pottery bowl; 1.9–3.1 h., 7.9 dm.; Level X, Floor 6, Court	Fig. 67:4
11 N 121	Miniature pottery bowl; medium fine, chaff-tempered, buff ware, cream slip, damaged, hole in bottom; 2.0 h., 4.85 dm.; Level X, Floor 4, Room 1	––
11 N 122	Miniature pottery jar; medium fine, chaff-tempered, greenish ware, cream slip; 4.4 h., 3.7 dm.; Level X, Floor 4, Room 1	Fig. 67:6
11 N 123	Miniature pottery jar with four feet; medium coarse, chaff-tempered, reddish ware, cream slip; 4.9 h., 4.4 dm.; Level X, Floor 4, Room 1	Fig. 67:7
11 N 124	Black stone weight; lentoid shape; weight 4.7 grams; 2.4 l., 0.8 dm.; Level X, Floor 4, Room 1	Fig. 68:1
11 N 130	Black stone cylinder seal, conflict among gods; Akkadian style; 1.95 h., 1.1 dm.; see Boehmer, *Die Entwicklung der Glyptik während der Akkad-Zeit* (Berlin, 1965) Nos. 311, 316; Level X, Floor 4, Court	Fig. 68:2
11 N 131	Soft white stone cosmetic dish with four compartments; 2.0 h., 6.8 w.; Level X, Floor 4, Court	Fig. 68:3
11 N 112	Damaged black stone cup; bitumen around edge of break indicates a repair in antiquity; 9.1 h., 10.0 dm.; Level X, Floor 3, Court, north corner, beside 11 N 117–20	Fig. 68:4
11 N 117	Small, complete, cracked pottery bowl; medium fine, chaff-tempered, buff ware, cream slip; 4.1 h., 13.9 dm.; Level X, Floor 3, Court, with 11 N 112, 118–20	Fig. 68:5
11 N 118	Small, complete, cracked pottery bowl; medium coarse, chaff-tempered, grayish ware, cream slip; 4.5 h., 16.7 dm.; Level X, Floor 3, Court, with 11 N 112, 117, 119, 120	Fig. 68:6

*Measurements are in centimeters.

FIELD NUMBER	DESCRIPTION	ILLUSTRATION
11 N 119	Fragmentary pottery bowl; same type as 11 N 118, but reddish ware; 5.4 h., 17.4 dm.; Level X, Floor 3, Court, with 11 N 112, 117, 118, 120	— —
11 N 120	Whole pottery bowl; same type as 11 N 118, but buff ware; 4.2 h., 14.3 dm.; Level X, Floor 3, Court, with 11 N 112, 117–19	— —
11 N 126	Fragment of shell cylinder seal; bull-man fighting lion; Akkadian; 2.6 h., 1.5 dm.; Level X, Floor 3, Court, in doorway	Fig. 68:7
11 N 127	White stone bowl fragment; 3.2 h., 10.4 dm. base; Level X, Floor 3, Court	Fig. 68:8
11 N 139	Damaged white stone cylinder seal; hero protecting animals; ED III; 2.8 h., 1.2 dm.; Level X, Floor 3, Room 1	Fig. 68:9
11 N 110	Damaged pottery jar; medium coarse, chaff-tempered, grayish ware, cream slip; contained copper objects (11 N 111); 9.8 h., 10.0 dm.; Level X, Floor 2, Area 1	Fig. 69:1
11 N 111	Copper objects found inside 11 N 110 (bent in antiquity to fit into jar): four discs, one flat rectangular piece, one needle, one wire, two bracelets, one ring(?), one bead (completely corroded), one fishhook	Fig. 69:2a–l
11 N 128	Fragment of baked-clay brick stamp with inscription: "Builder of the Temple of Enlil"; Naram-Sin; 6.7 h., 11.8 w., 3.5 th.; Level X, Floor 2, Area 1	Fig. 69:3

Level IX

11 N 97	White stone cylinder seal; hero, in long skirt, protecting animals; Akkadian or Post-Akkadian; 2.4 h., 0.35 dm.; Level IXc	Fig. 70:1
11 N 106	Hollow, baked-clay hedgehog figurine with incised lines indicating hair; 3.9 h., 7.2 l., 3.8 w.; Level IXc	Fig. 70:2
11 N 190	Pottery bowl; medium fine, chaff-tempered cream ware, cream slip, with incised lines below rim; shape is unusual for so early a date; 8.2 h., 11.9 dm.; Level IX, floor not certain	Fig. 70:3

Level VIII

11 N 165	Baked-clay weight(?) with two holes for suspension; 8.3 h., 7.0 w., 2.3 th.; see *Nippur* I, Pl. 153:2, for a similar object from Isin-Larsa context; Level VIII, southeast side, in baulk	Fig. 70:4
11 N 166	Fragmentary pottery jar; medium coarse, chaff-tempered, reddish ware, no slip; 14.2 h., 8.5 dm.; see *Nippur* I, Pls. 96:3, 95:7, for similar types	Fig. 70:5

FIELD NUMBER	DESCRIPTION	ILLUSTRATION
	in the Isin-Larsa/Old Babylonian range; Level VIII, southeast side, in baulk	

Burial Originating above Level VII

11 N 58	Complete pottery jar; medium coarse, chaff-tempered, buff ware, cream slip; 11.5 h., 8.1 dm.; see *Nippur* I, Pl. 98:5, Type 45; Burial 3, cut down into Level VII	Fig. 70:6
11 N 59	Complete pottery jar; fine, chaff-tempered, greenish ware, no slip; 15.4 h., 6.9 dm.; see *Nippur* I, Pl. 98:11, 12, Type 46A; Burial 3, cut down into Level VII	Fig. 70:7
11 N 60	Fragmentary pottery bowl; coarse, chaff-tempered, greenish ware, greenish slip; 11.5 h., 15.4 dm.; see *Nippur* I, Pl. 97:11, 12, Type 43C; Burial 3, cut down into Level VII; inverted over skull	Fig. 70:8

Level VI

11 N 167	Fragmentary pottery jar; medium fine, chaff-tempered, greenish ware, no slip; see *Nippur* I, Pl. 102:10; Level VI, in earth partially cut by firepit, therefore earlier than VId	Fig. 71:1
11 N 20	Fragmentary baked-clay monkey figurine; traces of red paint along arms and top of head; 6.9 h., 2.7 w., 4.3 th.; Level VI, above VId	Fig. 71:3
11 N 54	Fragmentary horse-and-rider figurine; very crude; 10.3 h., 11.7 l., 3.4 w.; Level VI, above VId	Fig. 71:2
11 N 193	Fragmentary pottery jar with pointed bottom and two lug handles; very coarse, chaff-tempered, buff ware, cream slip; decorated with incised vertical lines on body and raised and incised horizontal lines on neck; 36.0 h., 20.8 dm.; Level VIa	Fig. 71:4
11 N 55	Baked-clay bulla; lion walking to right, with crescent and lozenge above his back; filler below groundline may be a fish; 7.2 h., 6.7 w., 2.0 th.; trash pit cut into Level VI	Fig. 71:5

Intrusive into Level VI from Level V

11 N 22	Light-green glazed pottery jar; whole; fine, chaff-tempered cream ware; 9.5 h., 7.6 dm.; found with 11 N 23–31; Burial 1, cut into Level VI	Fig. 72:1
11 N 23	Light-green glazed pottery jar; whole; medium fine, chaff-tempered buff ware; 6.5 h., 7.6 dm.; found with 11 N 22, 24–31; Burial 1	Fig. 72:2
11 N 24	Unglazed pottery jar; complete; medium fine, chaff-tempered, buff ware, cream slip; 16.4 h., 13.2 dm.; found with 11 N 22, 23, 25–31; Burial 1	Fig. 72:3
11 N 25	Fragmentary pottery bowl; very fine buff ware, cream slip; 7.5 h., 12.4 dm.; found with 11 N 22–24, 26–31; Burial 1	Fig. 72:4

FIELD NUMBER	DESCRIPTION	ILLUSTRATION
11 N 26	Fragmentary copper bowl; 3.2 h., 8.5 dm.; found with 11 N 22–25, 27–31; Burial 1	Fig. 72:5
11 N 27	Corroded copper reticule with other objects fused to it; 9.2 l., 1.45 dm.; found with 11 N 22–26, 28–31; Burial 1	Fig. 72:6
11 N 28	Fragmentary polished-bone hairpin with decorated end; 10.0 l., 0.5 dm.; found with 11 N 22–27, 29–31; Burial 1	Fig. 72:7
11 N 29	Fragmentary polished-bone spatula; 6.2 l., 1.8 w., 0.15 th.; found with 11 N 22–28, 30–31; Burial 1	
11 N 30	Corroded copper ring; found with 11 N 22–29, 31; Burial 1	Fig. 72:9
11 N 31	Copper and shell beads; found with 11 N 22–30; Burial 1	Fig. 72:8
11 N 47	Light-green glazed pottery bottle; complete; medium fine, chaff-tempered, cream ware; 13.4 h., 11.7 dm.; found with 11 N 48–53; Burial 2, in pottery coffin, cut down into Level VI; this bottle was found in front of waist, with 11 N 48	Fig. 73:1
11 N 48	Green glazed pottery jar; broken; medium fine, chaff-tempered buff ware; 7.2 h., 7.5 dm.; found with 11 N 47, 49–53; Burial 2, in front of waist	Fig. 73:2
11 N 49	Unglazed pottery jar; rim missing; medium coarse, chaff-tempered, reddish ware, cream slip; 15.0 h., 13.7 dm.; found with 11 N 47, 48, 50–53; Burial 2, in front of chest	Fig. 73:3
11 N 50	Corroded, broken copper pin; 12.6 l., 0.4 dm.; Burial 2, at waist	Fig. 73:4
11 N 51	Polished-bone spatulas; broken; max. 12.0 l., ca. 2.0 w.; Burial 2, at knees	Fig. 73:5
11 N 52	Composite (frit?) beads (ten); 0.3–0.5 l., 0.35–0.4 dm.; Burial 2, at wrist and scattered	Fig. 73:6
11 N 53	Copper pendant; head of *puzuzu;* tang on bottom may have fitted into some other material to form whole body of the monster; 2.85 h., 0.8 w., 1.8 th.; Burial 2, under pelvis, perhaps originally hung from belt	Fig. 73:7

Level V

11 N 16	Fragmentary baked-clay female tambourine player wearing necklace and bracelets; 5.4 h., 5.9 w.; Level V, northern corner	Fig. 74:1
11 N 18	Fragmentary horse-and-rider figurine; 11.4 h., 9.4 l., 3.9 w.; Level V	Fig. 74:2

FIELD NUMBER	DESCRIPTION	ILLUSTRATION
Level IV		
11 N 15	Head from baked-clay horse figurine; 8.3 h., 2.5 w.; Level IV	——
Level I		
11 N 4	Fragmentary baked-clay female tambourine player wearing bracelet and necklace; 6.6 h., 5.0 w.; Level I	Fig. 74:3
11 N 5	Fragment of hollow, baked-clay female figurine; Hellenistic; 8.2 h., 6.9 w.; cf. Fig. 37:2, 3 for 11 N 89, 90, fragments of figurines made with same technique; Level I	Fig. 74:4
Fill above Level I		
11 N 1	Fragment of rider with cap turned down to left side of head, from horse-and-rider figurine; 6.8 h., 3.1 w.	——
11 N 2	Fragment of rider with pointed cap turned to front, from horse-and-rider figurine; 6.0 h., 2.0 w.	——

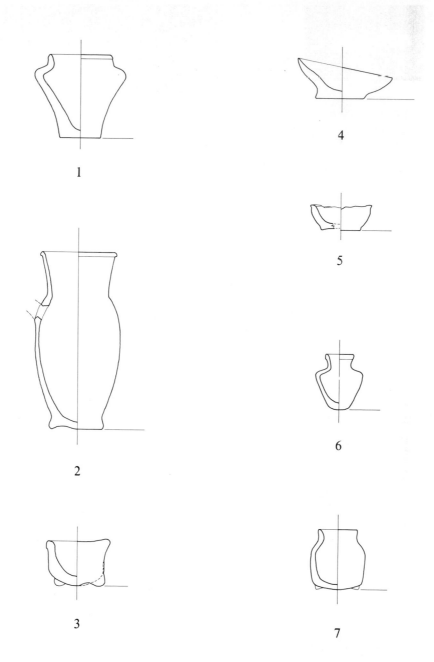

Fig. 67.—Pottery from WA 50*c*, Level X

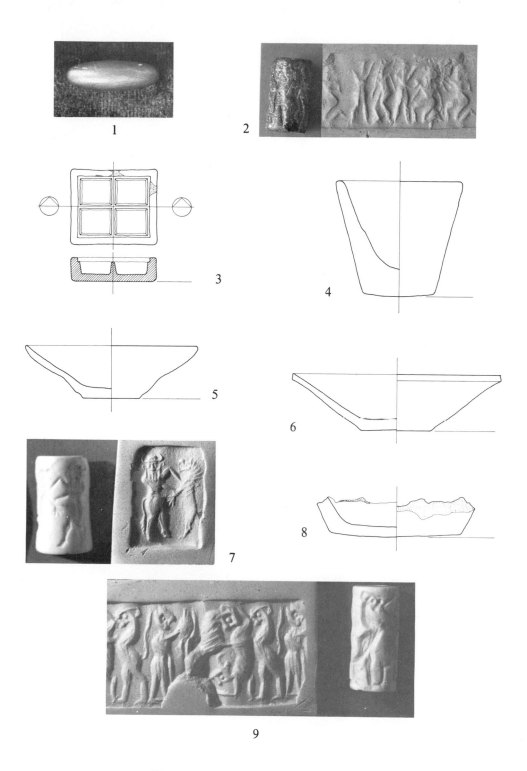

Fig. 68.—Objects from WA 50c, Level X

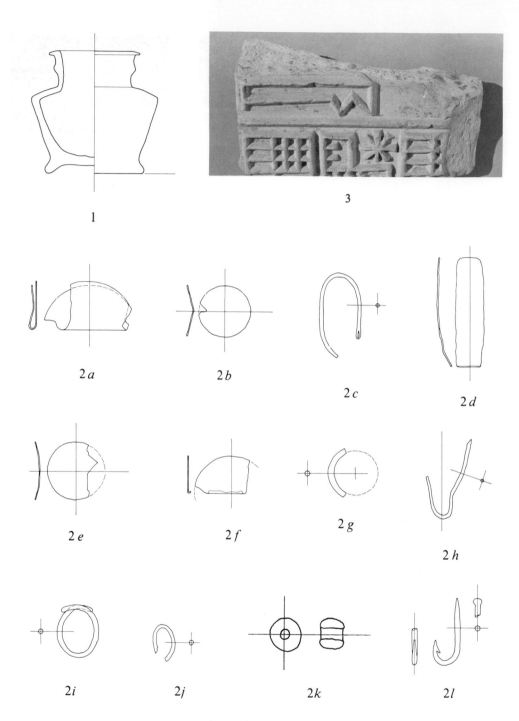

1

3

2 a

2 b

2 c

2 d

2 e

2 f

2 g

2 h

2 i

2 j

2 k

2 l

Fig. 69.—Objects from WA 50c, Level X

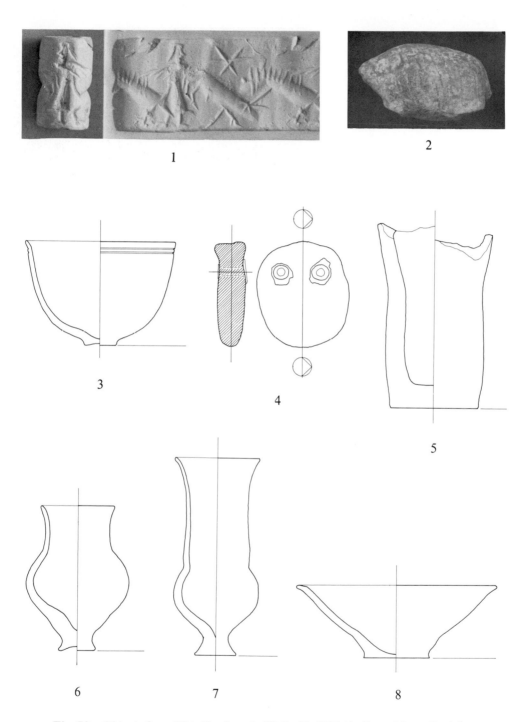

Fig. 70.—Objects from WA 50*c*, Levels IX (1—3), VIII (4—5), and from Burial 3 (6—8).

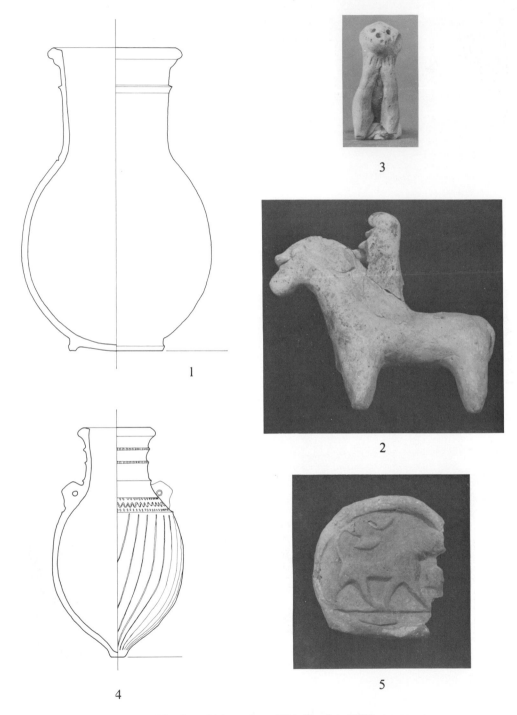

1

2

3

4

5

Fig. 71.—Objects from WA 50c, Level VI

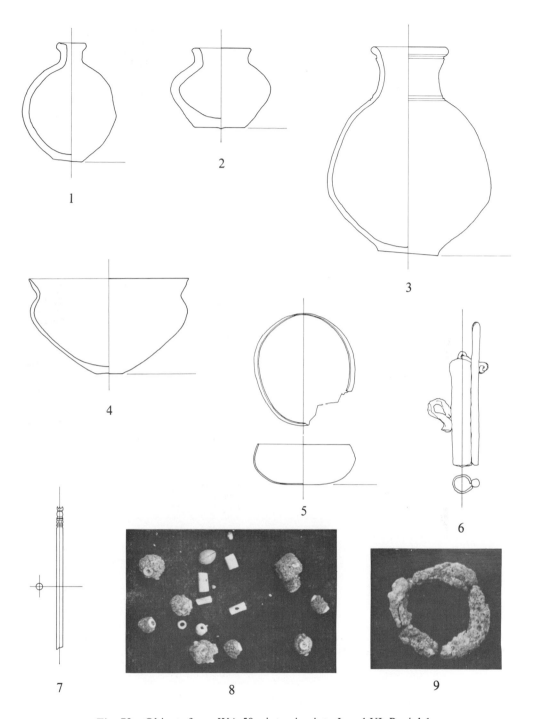

Fig. 72.—Objects from WA 50*c*, intrusive into Level VI, Burial 1

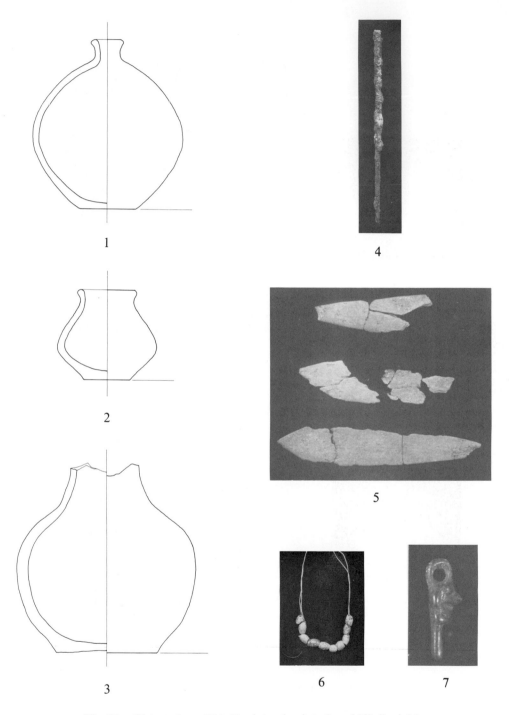

1

2

3

4

5

6

7

Fig. 73.—Objects from WA 50c, intrusive into Level VI, Burial 2

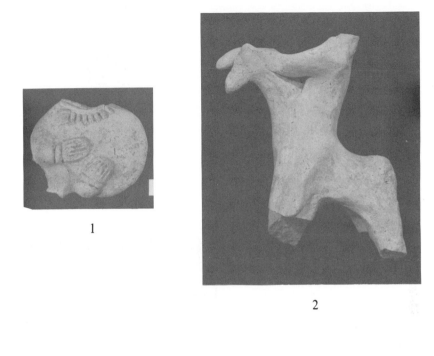

1

2

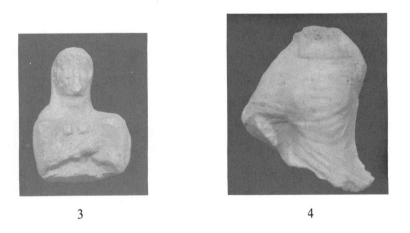

3

4

Fig. 74.—Objects from WA 50*c*, Levels V (1, 2) and I (3, 4)

IV

AREA WB

When we began working in WB in January, 1973, this area had the appearance of a high undisturbed knoll surrounded by very large Pennsylvania pits. Approaching WB from the south, up a slope (Fig. 75), one could see strata of ash, tamped floors, sherds, and the like. Since there was a slope, it was thought that we could employ a step trench and quickly recover good stratigraphy. Because the surface was littered with Kassite goblets, and since Pennsylvania in the 1890's had found Kassite material in the vicinity, WB seemed an especially advantageous place to work.

A grid of 6 × 10 m. units was laid out and numbered, WB 1 being at the crown of the hill. During the season, we were able to open all of WB 1 and 2, and a part of WB 4. We expect to expand this operation, especially to the east, in the coming seasons.

An hour of digging made it obvious that WB was not what it seemed and had, in fact, been investigated by Pennsylvania. There were extensive tunnels and trenches, descending as much as 4.5 m. The earlier excavators had heaped debris from nearby operations on their trenches. The east profile of WB 1 and 2 shows the state of the area as we found it (Figs. 76, 77).

The remains in WB seemed primarily residential. The building and rebuilding of walls upon the stubs of earlier walls made it very difficult to determine the history of this area, but a tentative reconstruction can be given.

At the bottom of our excavation, we reached a tamped earth floor (Level V) within mud-brick walls. We have dated this lowest set of walls and floor tentatively as Isin-Larsa (Fig. 78). The walls resting on Level V were preserved to a height of over a meter in places. These were foundations for walls with slightly different lines but following the same general room plan. This second phase of walling and the floors associated with it we designated Level IV. In most of the rooms excavated, Level IV actually comprised two or three rebuildings and realignments of walls in mud brick. One of the later rebuildings in Level IV was baked brick, a rarity in private houses. This unusual construction we can date by means of cuneiform tablets to the Old Babylonian Period. Whether the earlier phases of Level IV are also to be dated

Old Babylonian rather than Isin-Larsa is not yet certain. After the abandonment of the Old Babylonian buildings, the area seems to have lain unused.
Level III was a deliberate filling in preparation for a large, well constructed
building of Level II. We have tentatively dated Level II to the late second
millennium B.C. Level I, above this building, was too badly destroyed to give
dating indicators.

In the following description of levels, locus and room designations will be
presented as recorded. The rooms within the houses are being renumbered
and a uniform system will be adopted for future seasons. We keep the more
cumbersome system (e.g., WB 1, Room 3; WB 2, Room 3), so as to avoid
changing all our notes at this time.

The walls of Level V were composed of mud bricks measuring 25–26 ×
16–18 × 7–8 cm., and this size was standard also for the walls of Level IV.
This level, plus a single floor associated with it, was reached in only a few of
the rooms. A burial, enclosed in a corner of WB 2, Room 3, by means of a
row of mud bricks, had been disturbed in antiquity. A few scattered bones
and whole jar (11 N 99, Fig. 86:1) were all that remained of it. This burial
must have been put in when the house of Level V was abandoned and then
covered with the meter of fill within the foundation for Level IV.

Level IV was a complex set of rebuildings associated with well marked,
tamped earth and ash-strewn floors (Figs. 78, 79). The walls of Level IV
were somewhat less wide than the meter-high footings. At the earlier floors
of Level IV, the southern part of the area seems to have been the more
important and more intensively occupied. There were more ashy striations
between major floors in WB 2 than in WB 1, and the court (WB 1, 6)
seemed to be the focus of activity. At Floor 4, rooms in WB 1 were definitely
part of the WB 2 building. Access was had from the court, WB 1, 6, through
WB 1, 4 into the area to the northwest. Not enough was excavated in WB 1
to ascertain the nature of the northwestern area at Floor 4, but the dividing
wall (W) would seem to indicate rooms rather than a court.

At Floor 3, changes were made in parts of the structure. In WB 1, Room
4, a less substantial wall was built on the stub of the earlier Level IV wall.
Shortly thereafter, the doorways on the northwest and southeast walls of the
room were blocked (Fig. 81). Access must have been had through a wall to
the southwest. In WB 1, Rooms 3 and 5, a simultaneous blocking of a
doorway took place. The closing of these doorways marked the separation of
WB into two distinct living units. The more southern unit continued to be
used heavily. The toilet in WB 2, Room 2, and the mud-brick benches in WB
2, Room 6, which may have been potstands, indicate that the area we have
exposed was the more utilitarian, less formal part of a rather sizeable house.

In WB 1, the later phases of Level IV were as follows: After the closing of
the doorways in Rooms 3 and 4, there was a light occupation resulting in
one floor (Floor 2). Above this floor, there was more than 40 cm. of fill, laid
down prior to the construction of a house of baked bricks measuring 28 × 28
× 8 and 28 × 17 × 8 cm. This building was associated, essentially, with only

one floor, Level IV, 1. This floor was especially important because on it were found, especially in the courtyard, many artifacts as they had been left when the house was abandoned (Figs. 79, 82). Around and over pottery vessels, grindstones, and other items were about a dozen striations of sand lenses blown in over time and set in place, perhaps, by light rains. There was no violent destruction of the building. It seems merely to have gone out of use for a time and was then allowed to fall. The debris above the lenses of sand was composed of fragments of mud brick, plaster, and wind-blown sand. In places alongside the walls, the debris that washed down as the walls crumbled was very evident. This crumbling and washing down also occurred in WB 1, Room 5, where the result can be seen on the baulk (Fig. 77).

The baked-brick house and the house south of it were apparently abandoned at about the same time. The date of that abandonment can be estimated more definitely than is the case with most archeological levels. Several reconstructable pottery vessels that fit within the Old Babylonian range and a baked-clay plaque showing a man riding an animal (11 N 155, Fig. 87:2) helped to fix the buildings in time. But several cuneiform tablets found in the baked-brick courtyard and the small chamber northeast of it (WB 4, Room 2) gave a more precise dating. Below Floor 1 in the courtyard was found an Old Babylonian contract, which was done as a school exercise (Appendix A, No. 14). From above that floor in WB 4, Room 2 came two texts that deal with the distribution of large amounts of bread for various workmen and are dated to the 34th (Appendix A, No. 9) and 35th (Appendix A, No. 10) years of Hammurabi. Two more texts found in the same locus (Appendix A, Nos. 13, 15) are literary, but one (No. 13) is dated to the 10th or 11th year of Samsuiluna. Another tablet dated to the 13th year of Samsuiluna (Appendix A, No. 11) was found in fill above Floor 1 in the west corner of the courtyard along with an undated contract (Appendix A, No. 12). The latter document concerns the renting of a bed. A small baked-clay bead with a puzzling numerical inscription (Appendix A, No. 34) was also found above Floor 1 in the court. Dr. Civil indicates that the numbers are written in a style not known as early as Old Babylonian and questions the validity of the findspot. It is possible that the bead is intrusive from above, but our field notes state that the object came from Floor 1, under the sand lenses.

Given the written evidence, we can propose that the baked-brick building was constructed sometime before 1756 B.C., Hammurabi's 34th year, and was abandoned sometime after 1736 B.C., Samsuiluna's 13th year. The house that adjoins it was in use a number of years before 1756 B.C.

In the debris at about the top of the baked-brick walls of the court was found a Kassite tablet fragment dealing with the distribution of garments (Appendix A, No. 17). This tablet was accompanied by sherds of Kassite goblets. This material seems to have been deposited just before or as part of a deliberate filling and preparation (Level III) for a large building of Kassite or later age (Level II). The drain in the western end of the court was full of Kassite goblet sherds, and we have tentatively dated it and the building to that period. We hesitate to assign a firm date to the building since undisturbed evidence was almost completely lacking. The baked bricks in the pavement were so varied in size ($31 \times 31 \times 6.5$, $34 \times 34 \times 5.5$, $36 \times 36 \times 6.5$, $39 \times 39 \times 4.5$, $41.5 \times 41.5 \times 6$ cm.) that one must assume a reuse of earlier material. The size of the mud bricks ($33 \times 33 \times 11$ cm.) was similar to that of Level I or II mud bricks in WA. Further digging to the east will, hopefully, expose more of this structure.

The building was constructed in two phases. The earlier one (Fig. 83) had a doorway with a raised sill and drain (Fig. 85). The paving outside this wall, which perhaps originally ran to the wall at the northeast, may have been a street. At a later time, the surface rose, obscuring the paving and sill (Fig. 84). A new door socket of baked brick was set just inside the doorway at this time. Very heavy charcoal, ash, and reddened earth lying above Level IIa are evidence of a fire that may have destroyed the building.

Some floor lines above the stubs of the walls indicate a later level (I), but no dating can be attempted for it.

The findings in WB were very informative but were more indicative of a need for further work. We have called this a private-house area, but the tablets found here were in some cases classifiable as "administrative." Whether this word should be taken to imply administration by some central, governmental, or temple agency is open to question. There is mention in some texts of the Ninurta temple, but so far there is nothing specifically religious about the area. It may be that the baked-brick house was the residence either of a scribe or scribes working for that temple or of artisans on contract to it. The relationship of governmental bodies or religious entities to private groups, the existence or nonexistence of a scribal quarter rather than a sprinkling of scribes throughout the city wherever needed, and the evidence for business conducted from private houses may be clarified by our work in this area. We took many samples of soil from rooms and parts of rooms and from the inside of jars, and we hope that analyses will give an indication of the function of parts of the buildings. Notes were made of the location and sizes of sherds to show possible evidence of communication routes within the buildings. Such notations may allow us to suggest areas in which specific tasks were performed. The correlation of written documents with changes in houses, such as the blocking of doorways, may allow us to illustrate actual evidence of the sale and purchase of rooms. Likewise, the study of the content of tablets along with material found in houses may show that they vary together. In order to make possible such research, much more time and care were expended in this operation than would normally be given. The mass of sherds and artifacts was such that we were not able to analyze, type, draw, and otherwise deal with the sherds and some of the objects. A few objects were only drawn or photographed and stored at Nippur. Thus, for instance, some of the stone artifacts from the courtyard of WB 1/4 were not registered. On our return to Nippur, these items will be registered and incorporated with new-found material. A study of the sherds will appear in the final publication.

Fig. 75.—General view of Area WB, from the southeast before excavation

Fig. 76.—General view of Area WB, from the northwest late in the season

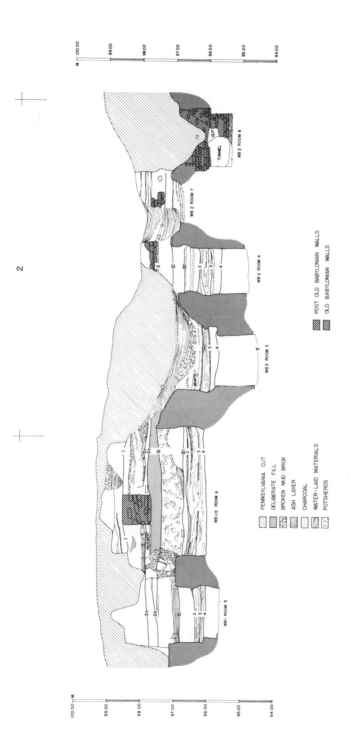

Fig. 77.—Section of east baulk of Area WB

109

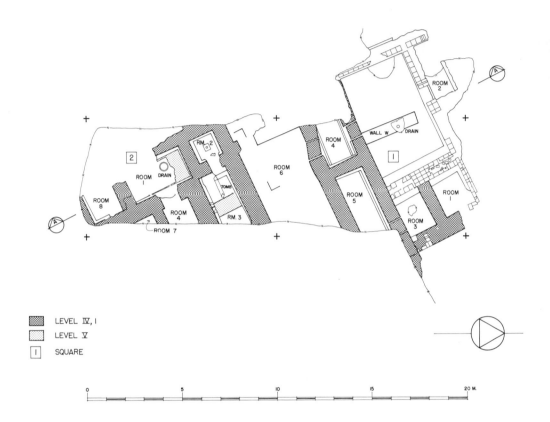

Fig. 78.—Plan of WB, Level V and lower part of Level IV

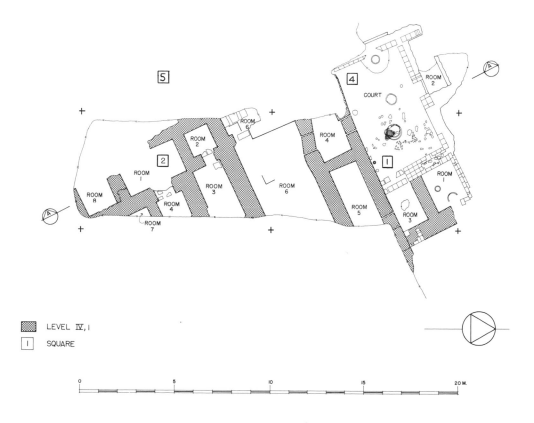

Fig. 79.—Plan of WB, Level IV, Floor 1

111

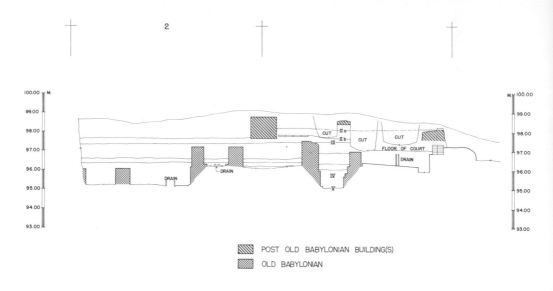

POST OLD BABYLONIAN BUILDING(S)

OLD BABYLONIAN

Fig. 80.—Section A-A of WB

Fig. 81.—Area WB 1, Room 4, showing blocking of doorway in southeast wall

Fig. 82.—Area WB 1/4, courtyard, Floor 1, debris *in situ* on floor, from the southeast.

POST OLD BABYLONIAN WALLS

SQUARE

| 0 | | 5 | | 10 | | 15 | | 20 M. |

Fig. 83.—Plan of WB, Level II*b*

113

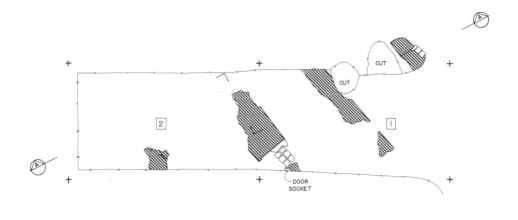

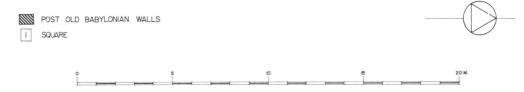

POST OLD BABYLONIAN WALLS

SQUARE

0 5 10 15 20 M.

Fig. 84.—Plan of WB, Level II*a*

Fig. 85.—Area WB, Level II*b*, from the northwest, showing drain built into doorway.

114

CATALOGUE OF OBJECTS
BY LOCUS AND LEVEL IN WB

FIELD NUMBER	DESCRIPTION*	ILLUSTRATION
Level V		
11 N 99	Pottery jar with rounded bottom and grooves at shoulder; whole; medium coarse, chaff-tempered, reddish ware, cream slip; 46.6 h., 15.4 dm. at rim; see *Nippur* I, Pl. 87:2; from Burial 3 in WB 2, Room 3	Fig. 86:1
Level IV		
11 N 189	Buff-ware pottery jar with groove at neck; complete; medium fine, chaff-tempered grayish ware, greenish slip; 27.4 h., 10.2 dm. at rim; see *Nippur* I, Pl. 95:10; WB 1, Room 5, high in fill just below Level IV, Floor 4	Fig. 86:2
11 N 176	Handmade, hollow, baked-clay figurine; man with lamb(?); 8.15 h., 3.55 w.; WB 1/4, fill below Floor 2 in courtyard	Fig. 86:3
11 N 188	Buff-ware pottery jar with ring base; medium fine, chaff-tempered reddish ware, cream slip; 17.5 h., 17.5 dm.; see *Nippur* I, Pl. 94:14; WB 1/4, fill below Floor 2 west of Wall W, where it joins southeast wall of court	Fig. 86:4
11 N 109	Fragmentary baked-clay figurine; torso with applied decoration; 3.4 h., 5.2 w., 1.55 th.; WB 1/4, Floor 1, court	Fig. 87:1
11 N 151	Round flat bead, brown stone with white flecks; 3.2 dm., 0.5 th.; WB 1/4, Floor 1, court	——
11 N 155	Baked-clay, mold-made plaque; man riding animal; 6.5 h., 5.2 w.; see *Nippur* I, Pl. 137:8; WB 1/4, Floor 1, court	Fig. 87:2
11 N 156	Black stone duck weight; 1.2 h., 2.0 l., 1.3 w.; WB 1/4, Floor 1, court	Fig. 87:3
11 N 157	Baked-clay bead with inscription; 1.1 dm., 0.45 th.; see Appendix A for discussion; WB 1/4, Floor 1, court	Fig. 87:4
11 N 160	Copper fish hook; 4.45 l.; WB 4, Room 2, Floor 1	——
11 N 154	Fragmentary baked-clay figurine; legs of nude female; 4.8 h., 3.2 w.; WB 1, Room 4, Floor 1	Fig. 87:5
11 N 158	Fragmentary "Kassite goblet"; medium coarse, chaff-tempered, greenish ware, no slip; 29.6 h., 8.8 dm.; WB 1/4, fill above sand lenses in court	Fig. 87:6
11 N 159	Fragmentary "Kassite goblet"; medium coarse, chaff-tempered, buff ware, cream slip; 29.6 h., 9.2 dm.; WB 1/4, fill above sand lenses in court	Fig. 87:7

*Measurements are in centimeters.

115

FIELD NUMBER	DESCRIPTION	ILLUSTRATION

Level III

11 N 137   Flat-based, broken pottery bowl with hole in bottom; coarse, chaff tempered, greenish ware, no slip; 10.7 h., 17.9 dm. rim; WB 1, in fill below wall of Level II   Fig. 87:8

Intrusive into Level IV from above Level III

11 N 41   Pottery jar; medium fine, yellowish ware, cream slip; 18.6 h., 16.4 dm.; disturbed Burial 1 cut into WB 2, Room 2, resting on Level IV, 2   Fig. 88:1

11 N 42   Fragmentary eggshell ware pottery bowl with lines incised at rim; 7.3 h., 11.9 dm.; same locus as 11 N 41   Fig. 88:2

Unstratified, from disturbed debris

11 N 39   Square pottery incense burner with four legs; incomplete; incised and impressed decoration; 9.8 h., 9.8 w.; see Fig. 34:2 for similar object; WB 1/4, disturbed fill   Fig. 88:3

11 N 57   Kidney-shaped pendant of green(?) glazed frit; glaze now almost white; 3.45 l., 2.3 w., 0.5 th.; WB 1/4, disturbed fill   Fig. 88:4

11 N 98   Head from baked-clay male figurine, with pellet eyes, turban and beard; 3.0 h., 2.5 w.; see *Nippur* I, Pl. 129:2, 5; WB 1/4, disturbed fill   Fig. 88:5

11 N 178   Baked-clay figurine of humped bull; 3.2 h., 4.1 l.; WB 1, Pennsylvania backfill   Fig. 88:6

11 N 103   Fragmentary baked-clay female figurine; 7.1 h., 4.0 w.; WB 4, Pennsylvania tunnel debris   Fig. 88:7

11 N 45   Bronze implement with spatulate ends; 14.7 l., 1.45 w. at ends; WB 2, disturbed fill   ——

11 N 197   Fragmentary baked-clay figurine of female on bed; 5.9 h., 4.0 w.; WB 5, disturbed fill   Fig. 88:8

11 N 56   Fragmentary baked-clay female figurine with applied eyes, etc.; 5.7 h., 5.0 w.; see *Nippur* I, Pl. 122:4, 10; WB, locus not specified, disturbed fill   Fig. 88:9

CATALOGUE OF OBJECTS FOUND OUTSIDE OF EXCAVATION AREAS

11 N 3   Fragmentary baked brick stamped with impression of bull walking to left; Assyrian; 24.3 h., 17.3 w., 7.0 th.; see Loud and Altman, *Khorsabad* II (Chicago, 1938) Pl. 65; found in bed of Shatt an-Nīl, north of WA   Fig. 89:1

11 N 6   White stone hoe; Ubaid-Jemdet Nasr; 11.0 l., 7.6 w., 2.4 th.; surface, West Mound   ——

FIELD NUMBER	DESCRIPTION	ILLUSTRATION
11 N 76	Fragmentary limestone finial for a column; 11.7 h., 17.1 dm.; found by guard on small Early Islamic mound about a hundred meters north of the West Mound	Fig. 89:2
11 N 77	Whole pottery incantation bowl with 5 or 6 lines of Jewish script and figure of monster; 6.5 h., 16.0 dm.; see Appendix C below; found upside down on West Mound, about one hundred meters east of WA 50c; near 11 N 78	Fig. 89:3
11 N 78	Whole pottery incantation bowl with 7 or 8 lines of Jewish script; 5.5 h., 13.3 dm.; see Appendix C, below; same locus as 11 N 77	Fig. 89:4
11 N 104	Fragment of incantation bowl with three lines of Aramaic inscription; 3.2 h., 5.4 w.; surface; brought in by workmen	Fig. 89:5
11 N 113	Copper bull figurine; details like those in large-scale Achaemenid sculptures; 1.3 h., 1.9 l., 0.6 w.; found on surface of West Mound, near WA 50c	Fig. 90:1a−c
11 N 114	Fragment of hollow, nude male figurine; Hellenistic; 8.6 h., 6.7 w.; surface; brought in by workmen	Fig. 90:2
11 N 115	Crude baked-clay horse-and-rider figurine; rider made separately and attached to horse; 9.4 h., 8.5 l., 3.7 w.; surface; brought in by workmen	——
11 N 129	White stone bowl fragment inscribed in Sumerian; 3.0 h., 3.65 w., 1.2 th.; see Appendix A, below; surface, near Ekur; found by foreman	——
11 N 132	Fragment of black stone cylinder seal depicting goddess, nude female and demon; Old Babylonian; 2.1 h., 1.2 dm.; surface, West Mound; brought in by workman	Fig. 90:3
11 N 141	Fragmentary nude female figurine; nursing child; 9.5 h., 3.5 w., 2.7 th.; surface; brought in by workman	Fig. 90:4
11 N 142	Miniature pottery jar with pointed base; 6.8 h., 5.2 dm.; surface; brought in by workman	——
11 N 161	Flat, ovoid, greenish object, perhaps a bulla; 1.8 × 1.6 w., 0.8 th.; surface, West Mound	——
11 N 162	Copper stamp seal with lug for suspension; flat seal face too eroded to identify design; 1.0 h., 1.6 dm.; surface, West Mound	Fig. 90:5a−b
11 N 170	Damaged miniature pottery bowl; 2.1 h., 4.9 dm.; surface, West Mound	——
11 N 187	Copper coin; badly corroded; horned horse on obverse, anchor(?) on reverse; Seleucid; 1.6 dm., 0.3 th.; surface, West Mound, near expedition house	——

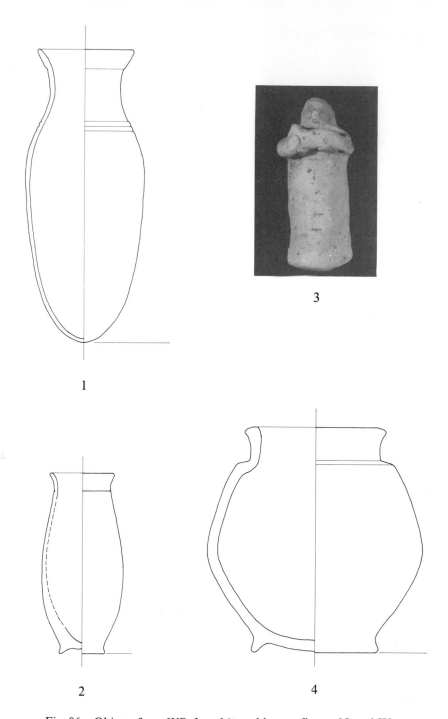

1

3

2

4

Fig. 86.—Objects from WB, Level V and lowest floor of Level IV

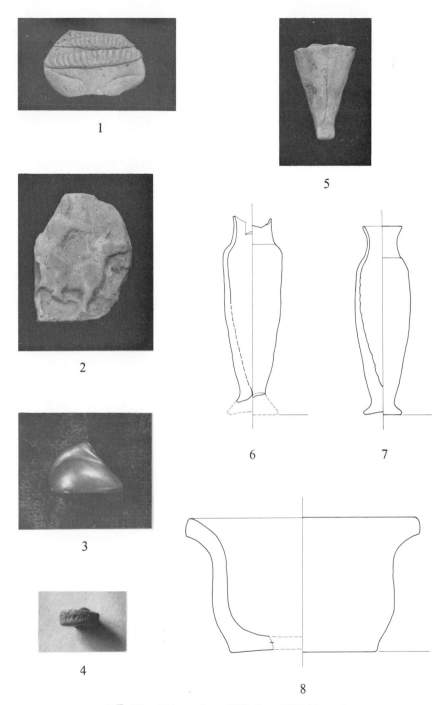

Fig. 87.—Objects from WB, Level IV, Floor 1

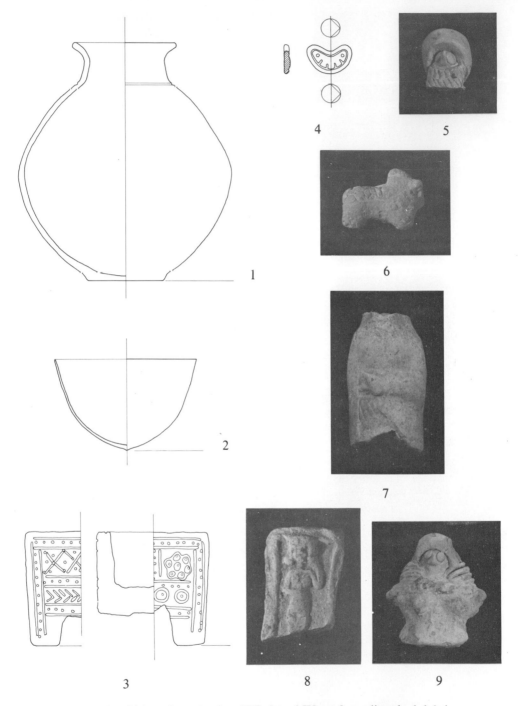

1

2

3

4

5

6

7

8

9

Fig. 88.—Objects intrusive into WB, Level IV, or from disturbed debris

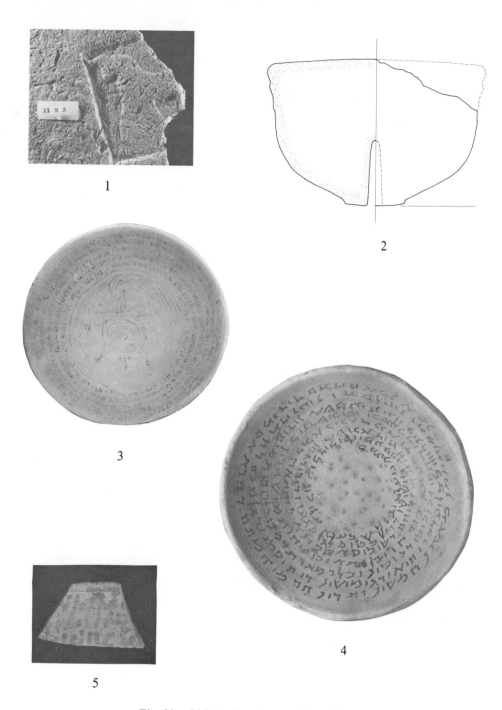

1

2

3

4

5

Fig. 89.—Objects found on surface of site

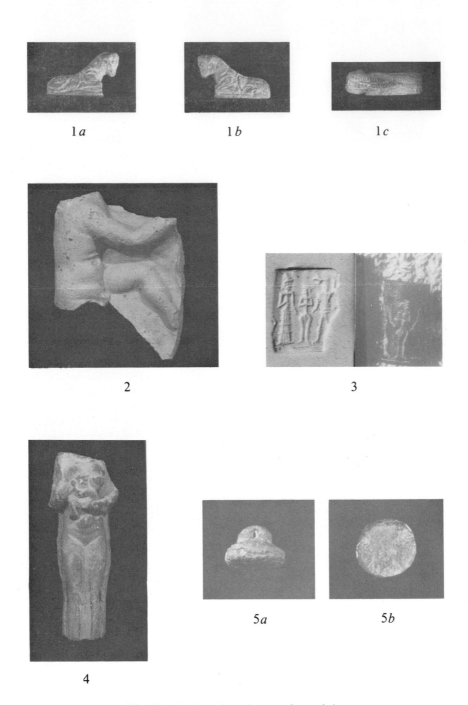

1a   1b   1c

2   3

5a   5b

4

Fig. 90.—Objects found on surface of site

V

CONCLUSIONS AND PROSPECTS

The results of this first season on the West Mound may be summed up briefly as follows: we have only begun to uncover a complex of temples in WA; we have added something definite to our understanding of the Akkadian Period in WA 50c; and we have succeeded in exposing a set of rooms in WB that will hopefully become a large exposure of houses with material well enough preserved and sufficiently recorded to allow reconstructions of social patterns not usually attempted in Mesopotamia.

The work in WA must become as large-scale an operation as the problem we face. If this complex of temples is anything like the Inanna Temple, with its multiple rebuildings, we could spend several seasons on this area alone. The working out of even the three or four levels we have now will be a time-consuming task. We must move the dune from above the temples and deal with whatever Seleucid and Parthian remains Pennsylvania left us. The continuation of the search for Kassite levels will go on here. It is hoped that at some point we may cut toward the east or northeast and examine the riverside.

Whether we do more work in the vicinity of WA 50c is doubtful for the time being. However, the Akkadian material and the fairly rich Achaemenid and Seleucid levels would make the cutting away of meters of eroded debris worthwhile.

Our work in WB during the next season will concentrate on exposing a much larger area of Old Babylonian houses in preparation for deeper trenches in subsequent years. In WB there is no problem of overburden, nor of possible water level problems when we reach early material. Here we are well above the plain, even in the lowest level we have reached.

If one compares Level IV in WB with Level VII in WA 50c and the very bottom of Level V in WA 12–13, all of which we have called Old Babylonian, the difference in elevation is striking. Old Babylonian levels in Tablet Hill were two or three meters lower than Level IV in WB. It is clear that Nippur was a city of depressions and rises, and that fairly early material may be found almost anywhere on the mound. The surprising height at which

such material is located on the southern end of the West Mound would indicate that this area had a long history of occupation in the early periods. A
series of search trenches must be made in various parts of the site to allow a
reconstruction of the growth and decline of the city.

The continuation of research at Nippur will gradually become the focus
for a wider, regional assessment of the city in its natural and topographic setting. The relationship of the city to villages and towns around it, to other
great cities, and to large political units should be investigated through a
combination of surveys, subsidiary soundings at neighboring sites, and study
of written records. In short, it is hoped that Nippur can continue as a center
for research into a variety of problems by a number of scholars.

APPENDIX A: CUNEIFORM TEXTS

by Miguel Civil

I. TABLETS

Sargonic

No. 1, 11 NT 19. WA 50*c* X, Room 1, Floor 4. 44 × 32 × 7 mm.; complete. Found with No. 2.

List of date growers (santana) of Enlil, with the number of baskets assigned to them.

	1 dusu MIN	1 basket ...
	lugal-itu-da	Lugalituda
	1 mu-zu-d[a]	1: Muzuda
	1 lugal-maḫ$_x$(AL)	1: Lugalmaḫ
5	1 níg-ᵈen-líl	1: Nig-Enlil
	2 ᵈen-líl-dingir-zu	2: Enlildingirzu
	1 santana	1: Santana
	šu-nigin₂ 7 dusu MIN	Total: 7 baskets ...
	santana ᵈen-líl-lá	Gardeners of Enlil
10	maškim lugal-[REC 56]	Agent: Lugal-X

Baskets designated as dusu (ÍL) for dates and occasionally other fruits are well known in the Ur III texts: see Fish, "Some Ur III Tablets from Lagash," *Archiv Orientální* XVII (1949) 227, where the capacity is given as from 12 to 16⅔ sila; note, however, that Lau, *Old Babylonian Temple Records* (New York, 1906) No. 141:1 ff. (not quoted by Fish) goes as high as 30 and as low as 10 sila. It is unlikely that MIN designates here the capacity, since it is not followed by sila. It could designate some type of basket. The gardeners are designated by the archaic logogram GAL.NI = santana(k) (ED Lu A, *MSL* XII 10, l. 22), a compound of sag + an unknown element; see Landsberger "Die Liste der Menschenklassen im babylonischen Kanon," *Zeitschrift für Assyriologie,* Vol. 41 (1933) pp. 189 f. It is not yet clear whether the difference between a santana and a nu-ᵍⁱˢkiri₆(SAR) is one of activities or authority; in any case, the santana is constantly associated with the cultivation of the date palms. Line 7: note the use of santana as a personal name; the practice of designating a person with the name of a profession is widespread in the Sargonic lists. Line 10: the last sign is uncertain, but REC 56 seems to fit the traces best.

No. 2, 11 NT 18. WA 50*c* X, Room 1, Floor 4. 44 × 32 × 7 mm. Left edge broken off.

List similar to No. 1; most of the names are repeated in lines 5 ff.

No. 3, 11 NT 17. WA 50*c* X, Room 1, Floor 4. 42 × 34 × 12 mm. Reverse uninscribed.

Unfinished tablet listing small amounts of metals, followed by personal names. For a-KA-dù, line 4, see Civil, "From Enki's Headaches to Phonology," *JNES,* Vol. 32 (1973) pp. 58 f.

No. 4, 11 NT 16. WA 50*c* X, Room 1, Floor 4. 50 × 36 × 14 mm. Most of the reverse is destroyed.

List of sheep and wool (sig-àk = *itqu,* "fleece," line 5).

Ur III

No. 5, 11 NT 1. WB 2, Pennsylvania dump. 30 × 28 mm. Obverse broken off. Not copied.

Only date preserved: itu apin-du$_8$-a, u$_4$ 28 zal-la, mu ús-sa ki-maš^{ki} ba-ḫul, mu ús-sa-bi (Šulgi 48/8/28).

No. 6, 11 NT 13. WB 2, south baulk, loose fill in Pennsylvania trench. 36 × 34 × 16 mm. Lower half, with only a few signs on the obverse preserved. Not copied.

Account of agricultural work: barley for seed, to feed the plowing oxen, and for the workers. Rev.: še-numun-bi 3 + [. . . (gur) . . .] ⅔ sila$_3$, šu-nigin$_2$ 32 gud UD [. . .], še-numun-bi 3.164 + [x], šu-nigin$_2$ 725 guruš u$_4$ [x-šè], á guruš 1-a 5 sila$_3$-t[a], še-bi [. . . gur], rest broken.

No. 7, 11 NT 12. WB 2, found together with No. 6. 38 × 30 mm. Chip from the left edge. Not copied.

Fragment of a níg-kas$_x$(ŠID)-ak account, dealing with grain. Only beginning of five lines preserved: sag-níg-[ga-ra-kam], šà-bi-[ta], etc.

No. 8, 11 NT 23. WB 2, found together with No. 6. 31 × 32 mm. Lower left corner, reverse only preserved. Not copied.

End of a ba-zi account, dealing with grain. Date: [mu ^{d}gu-za (erasure) ^{d}e[n-líl ba-dím] (Amar-Sin 3).

Old Babylonian

No. 9, 11 NT 29. WB 4, Room 2, Level IV, fill above Floor 1. 36 × 30 × 29 mm. Complete, with a portion of the envelope (not copied) with the seal partly preserved. Found with No. 10.

Distribution of bread rations for potters. Hammurabi 34, 3/1—4/1.

> 5 sila$_3$ ninda
> kurum$_6$ ⌈ur-du$_6$-kù-ga⌉ baḫar
> kurum$_6$ ku$_5$-da
> sá-dug$_4$ ninda ^{d}nin-urta-ke$_4$
> 5   itu šu-numun-a u$_4$-1-ta
> mu ḫa-am-mu-ra-bi [lugal]
> an ^{d}inanna ^{d}na-na-a-⌈a⌉
> e-ne-bi-ta
> 5 sila$_3$ kurum$_6$ arad-^{d}sin baḫar
> 10   kurum$_6$ ku$_5$-da

sá-dug₄ ninda ᵈnin-urta-ke₄
itu sig₄-a u₄-1-t[a]
mu ḫa-am-mu-ra-b[i lugal]
an ᵈinanna [ᵈna-na-a-a]
15   e-ne-bi-[ta]
Seal: i-bi-ᵈen-líl
      dub-sar

"5 silas of bread, food allowance of Ur-dukuga, the potter. The allowance is a portion from the sá-dug offerings of bread for Ninurta" (same formula for the potter Arad-Sin).

Line 2 is restored from the envelope. In line 4, the envelope has a -ne after -ke₄.

No. 10, 11 NT 28. WB 4, Room 2, Level IV, fill above Floor 1. 43 × 32 × 19 mm. Complete. Found with No. 9.

Distribution of bread rations and sheep for workers. Hammurabi 35/2/2–16. No seal visible.

5 ninda gur
GÌR ᵈsin-i-din-nam uku-uš
lú ⁱᵈi-šar-tum
ba-al-e-dè
5   30 (sila₃) ninda-ta 2 ma-la-kum udu
kurum₆ 3 kù-dím-me
lú ᵍⁱˢbanšur ᵈnin-urta
guškin gar-ra
ninda u₄ 15-kam
10   ninda-bi 1.150 (gur) 3 udu-[BALAG-ma]
      šu-nigin₂ 6.150 (gur) ninda
      3 udu-BALAG-ma
[ki]šib ip-qú-é-a
inim-gar-ᵈnin-urta ba-zi
15   itu gud-si-su u₄ 2-ta u₄ 16-šè
mu ḫa-am-mu-ra-bi lugal-e
inim ᵈen-líl-lá-ta
[bà]d má-ríᵏⁱ mà-al-[giₓᵏⁱ]
mu-un-gul

"5 gur of bread
through Sin-iddinam, the soldier,
for the men who had to dig the Išartum canal.
30 silas of bread each, (and) 2 sheep tongues,
food allowance for three goldsmiths,
who covered with gold Ninurta's table.
It is the bread for 15 days.

> Their bread is 1,150 gur, (and) 3 . . . sheep.
>   Total: 6,150 gur of bread
>   3 . . . sheep
>
> Seal of Ipqu-Ea.
> (The food) was taken out by Inimgar-Ninurta.
> Month of gud-si-su, from the 2d to the 16th day,
> Year when Hammurabi, by order of Enlil, destroyed
>   the walls of Mari and Malgi."

Line 3: ᴵᵈi-šar-tum = ŠU, Hh. XXII 4 21; Nippur Forerunner, l. 350; mentioned in the date Gungunum 22.

Line 5: Compare x UDU y UZU *ma-la-ku* (y ⟩ x) in Mari texts: J. Bottéro, *Textes économiques et administratifs* (*ARMT* VII [1957]) No. 206:1, 3, 3 ′, M. Birot, *Textes administratifs de la salle 5 du palais* (*ARMT* XII [1964]) No. 747:17, 27; cf. also *ARMT* VII 256. A part of the tongue according to Hh. XV 79, and its Hg. Commentary.

Line 10: For the unusual udu-BALAG-ma, later written udu-dìm-ma = *takmesu*, see Landsberger, *MSL* VIII/1 16, l. 96, and Oppenheim, "The Domestic Animals of Ancient Mesopotamia," *JNES* IV (1945) 161 and n. 78. Context occurrences are: C. Jean, *Contrats de Larsa* (Musée du Louvre, "Textes cunéiformes" X [Paris, 1926]) No. 100:25, 31; O. R. Gurney, "Texts from Dur-Kurigalzu," *Iraq* XI (1949) 145, No. 5:7; R. F. Harper, *Assyrian and Babylonian Letters*, Part VI (London, 1902) No. 634 rev. 1.

No. 11, 11 NT 21. WB 1/4, Level IV, Court, west corner, 10–20 cm. above Floor 1. 31 × 31 × 12 mm. Most of the obverse destroyed. Not copied.

Account (ba-zi), subject uncertain. Samsuiluna 13/1/1.

Only the date is well preserved; on the obv. PAD and [ba]-zi can be recognized. Date: mu ús-sa kur gú-ke₄.

No. 12, 11 NT 20. WB 1/4, Level IV, Court, west corner, 10–20 cm. above Floor 1. 23 × 23 × 14 mm. Complete. Traces of a seal impression showing a male figure on left, facing left, and a female figure on right, facing right.

Contract about hiring a bed. No date.

> *iš-tu* ITU APIN.DU₈.A U₄.1.KAM
> ᵐ*Warad-*ᵈ*nin-šubur*
> ᵍⁱˢNÁ
> ᵐ*be-el-š[u-n]u*
> 5½ ŠE KÙ.[BABBAR]
> IN.ḪUN.GÁ

"From the first day of the eighth month, Warad-Ninšubur rented a bed from Belšunu for 5½ grains of silver."

No. 13, 11 NT 31. WB 4, Level IV, Room 2 fill above Floor 1. Lower right corner. Calendar of uncertain nature, perhaps cultic. Samsuiluna 11(?), see below.

The preserved part consists of lines ending in month names followed by one or two lines, ending in ᵈsin ì-UD, except in lines 10′, [. . .]-[x] ì-DI, and 19′, [. . .]-ḪI(?) ì-UD. It is possible that, in the moderately cursive script of the tablet, all UD signs were intended as DI, but it seems unlikely. The months are not listed in their normal order, but, as far as the text is preserved, in the succession: [. . .], VII, I, II, VIII, [. . .], XII; there was room enough for every month of the year in the complete tablet. The cultic purpose, festivals or rotation of temple duties, is suggested by [. . .] ezen-ma before the month names, more or less preserved in lines 9′, 11′, and 16′, and by [. . . b]ala-gub-ba in 12′. The last word in line 20′: i-da-ma-ra-aṣ is part of the date (Samsuiluna 10 or 11).

No. 14, 11 NT 32. WB 1/4, Level IV, Court, northeast part, below Floor 1. 82 × 63 × 29 mm. Upper edge missing.
Model contract.

> (from two to four lines missing)
> [. . .] [x x x]
> [ki ᵐna]-bi-ᵈen-líl-ta
> ᵐᵈutu-ba-an-è-[k]e₄(?)
> šu ba-an-ti
> 5′ ša SAL.ÁŠ.KI(?) [x-x-(x)]-ka
> 1 gur-e ba-tur-re(-)ma [x x (x)]
> ub-ta-an-zi
> 30 gur še-eštub
> 20 gur še-muš₅
> 10′ [ka]r-r[a] nibruᵏⁱ-k[a]
> [š]e-bi al-ág-e
> [tuk]um-bi
> [ka]r-ra nibruᵏⁱ-ka
> š[e-b]i la-ba-an-ág-e
> 15′ K[I.LA]M-ka x
> a[l]-du-a-ginₓ
> k[ù-b]i ì-lá-e
> lú ki-inim-ma-
> k[a] mu-bi
> (useless traces of a few signs)

"[. . .] Utu-bane has received from Nabi-Enlil.
From the supplies(?) he will deduct one gur (of grain).
After having withdrawn (this amount),
he will deliver the grain: 30 gur of early grain and
30 gur of late grain, in the quay of Nippur.
If he does not deliver the grain, he will pay in silver
at the rate prevalent in the city(!). Witnesses: their names."

The formula lú ki-inim-ma mu-bi (18 ′ f.) classifies unmistakably this text as a "model contract." This genre of texts uses also the same formula for the date: itu-bi mu-bi (e.g. in A 33433). One or possibly several collections of model contracts can be reconstructed from a large number of Nippur tablets and fragments. No. 14 differs, however, in several respects from the typical model contract: its format and paleography are unusual for this genre, and there are glosses (lines 5 ′ f.) as well as traces of some undecipherable lines after the end of the contract proper (perhaps the scribe's name). If the doubtful sign at the end of line 3 ′ is really -[k]e₄, it is incorrect. The major difficulty is in lines 5 ′ f. On the surface it looks like the well-known formula šà GN^ki-ka, but the verb in the following line suggests a different inter-pretation along the lines of Ana ittišu IV iv 20: šà ka-kéš-da é-a bí-ib-tur-re : ina libbi kiṣir bīti uṣaḫḫar, "he will deduct from the rent of the house." Un-fortunately, I cannot offer any completely satisfactory solution for the read-ing of line 5 ′. The less far-fetched is to take SAL.ÁŠ and the following sign which has an outline like KI but could be also kár (GÁN-tenû), as an irregu-lar spelling for is-gar/éš-gàr (iškaru). The gloss may be read as ša-[kar]. Note that the reading zeḫ for SAL.ÁŠ.GAR in Proto-Ea, l. 432 is incorrect and that the logogram must be read ešgar (for details see the forthcoming revi-sion of Proto-Ea in *MSL* XIV). The lack of the opening lines in No. 14 pre-vents testing this interpretation of line 5 ′ f. Line 9 ′: the grain še-muš₅, almost always next to še-eštub, is unusual but not unknown in administrative texts; cf. M. Allotte de la Fuÿe, *Documents présargoniques* (Paris, 1908—20) No. 559 iii 9; *Vorderasiatische Schriftdenkmäler der Königlichen Museen zu Berlin* XIV (Leipzig, 1916) No. 170 obv. 4 ff.; Nikolski, *Dokumenty Kho-ziaistvennoi otchetnosti* (St. Petersburg, 1908) No. 87:1; H. de Genouillac, *Textes de l'époque d'Agadé et de l'époque d'Ur* ("Inventaire des tablettes de Tello" II/2 [Istanbul, 1911]) No. 3052 (p. 13); CBS 8180 rev. 1 (T. Fish, "The Sumerian City Nippur in the Period of the Third Dynasty of Ur," *Iraq* V (1938) 173. The last sign in line 15 ′ looks like a GÁN or GIŠ-tenû, but the context requires uru or kar.

No. 15, 11 NT 30. WB 4, Level IV, Room 2, fill above Floor 1. 112 × 61 × 26 mm.; complete, but surface damaged in several places.

Sumerian literary text: Edubba D, lines 65—100.

Composition 5.14 in the Chicago Sumerian Literary Catalogue (to be pub-lished as *Handbuch der Keilschriftliteratur* IV); incipit: lú-tur dumu é-dub-ba-me-en; 169 lines. Published sources: Chiera, *Sumerian Epics and Myths* ("Oriental Institute Publications" XV [Chicago, 1934]) No. 67, A. Goetze, "Texts and Fragments 9—11," *Journal of Cuneiform Studies* IV (1950) 137, Ni. 9498 (Çığ and Kızılyay, *Sumerian Literary Texts and Fragments* I [An-kara, 1969] 228 [Pl. 170]), Ni. 9718 (Kramer, Kızılyay, and Çığ, "Selected Su-merian Literary Texts," *Orientalia*, n.s., Vol. 22 [1953] Pl. 42), *UET* VI, No. 167; unpublished sources: CBS 2201 + N 3075 + N 3129, N 1241 (perhaps part of *Sumerian Epics and Myths*, No. 67), CBS 11786, CBS 13872, Ni. 4299, Ni. 9618, Ni. 9809 (all Ni. numbers to appear in *Sumerian Literary*

Texts and Fragments II), and UM 29-15-573. A reproduction of 11‚NT 30 will be found in the forthcoming edition of the text by M. Civil.

No. 16, 11 NT 33. WA 12, Level V, Room 2, below Floor 12. 31 × 28 × 16 mm. Lower left corner broken, surface severely damaged, rev. uninscribed.

Probably administrative text; only [. . .]-[x]-ti-ni is readable (line 1); all other traces uncertain. Could be MB. Not copied.

Kassite and Middle Babylonian

No. 17, 11 NT 15. WB 1, Level III(?), Court, north corner, in ancient debris near top of OB wall. 20 × 52 × 20 mm. Center fragment. Kassite.

Administrative text: list of garments.

No. 18, 11 NT 26. WA 12, Room 1, ash levels above Floor 12. Lenticular, diameter 60 mm.; one half missing. Kassite.

School exercise tablet: obv. list of reed objects; rev. unidentifiable traces, not copied.

$$^{gi}gakkul_x(\text{written DIM})\text{-}a\text{-}ab\text{-}ba$$
$$^{gi}gakkul_x\text{-}[a]$$
$$^{gi}gakkul\text{-}ka\check{s}$$
$$^{gi}A\check{S}\text{-}GIR\text{-}lum$$
$$5 \quad ^{gi}A\check{S}\text{-}du_8\text{-}a$$
$$^{gi}al(?)\text{-}BI\text{-}[x]$$

For ll. 1 ff., cf. *MSL* VII, No. 191:108 f.; for l. 4, TH ix 8 (quoted in *MSL* VII).

No. 19, 11 NT 27. WB, north edge, in disturbed debris. 31 × 39 × 18 mm.; complete.

Barley loan, with two witnesses, and *sissiktu* of the borrower. No date. Paleographically unusual for the Kassite period.

1 ŠE.UR₅.RA (GUR)	1 gur of barley, as a loan
GIŠ.BAR PAD	measure of the rations
ŠU.TI *ha-ha-sa-ah*	received by Hahasah.
*ši-bu gi-mil-*ᵈ*gu-la*	Witness: Gimil-Gula
*ši-bu ra-ba-ša-*ᵈ*nin-urta*	Witness: Raba-ša-Ninurta.
si-si-ik-ti	Impression of the fringe
ha-ha-sa-ah	of Hahasah('s garment).

Neo-Babylonian and Later

No. 20, 11 NT 3. WA 50*c* VI. 94 × 65 × 18 mm.; complete, baked.

Commentary to a therapeutic text (Köcher, *Die babylonische-assyrische Medizin in Texten und Untersuchungen* III [Berlin, 1964] No. 248 and dupl.). Colophon: *ṣa-a-ti šu-ut* KA *u maš-ʾ-al-ti šá* KA *um-man-nu šá* ŠÀ / én munus ù-tu-ud-da-a-ni IM.GÍD.DA ᵐᵈ50.KÁD / LÚ UŠ.KU ᵈ*en-líl* A *šá* ᵐᵈ*en-líl*-MU-*im-bi* ŠÀ.BAL.BAL / ᵐ*lú-dumu-nun-na šu-me-ru-ú*.

Found with Nos. 21 and 22. The three tablets have been published in M. Civil, "Medical Commentaries from Nippur," *JNES*, Vol. 33 (1974) pp. 329 ff., where further information about these tablets may be found.

No. 21, 11 NT 4. WA 50*c* VI. 55 × 42 × 13 mm.; complete, baked.
Twenty-fourth *pirsu* of a therapeutic commentary (*bulṭu É da-bi-bi*). Colophon: 24 *pir-su bul-ṭu É da-bi-bi* NU.AL.TIL / DIŠ NA MURUB₄.MEŠ-*šú* KÚ.MEŠ-*šú* / DIŠ NA *ina* KÀŠ-*šú* BAD *ú-tab-ba-kam* / IM.GÌ.DA ᵐᵈ*en-líl*-KÁD LÚ UŠ.KU ᵈALIM / lú dingir-bi ᵈnuška-ke₄.
See No. 20.

No. 22, 11 NT 5.* WA 50*c* VI. 26 × 24 mm.; small fragment from obv. center.
Commentary similar to Nos. 20 and 21.
See No. 20.

No. 23, 11 NT 14.* WA 7 V, Room 1, fill. 41 × 41 × 15 mm. Center fragment. Not copied.
Exercise tablet, lexical: Hh. X 227–38 (see *MSL* VII 88 f.); only end of col. i preserved; col. ii blank in lines 227–35; col. ii, l. 237: É.[MEŠ]; line 238: *pa*-[. . .]; omits line 237*a–f.* No variants.

No. 24, 11 NT 25. WA 8, fill under Wall C. 29 × 42 × 23 mm. Fragment of the upper edge of a large tablet. Not copied.
Lexical: Syllabary Sᵃ; obv. one unidentifiable line; rev. = lines 42–46.

No. 25, 11 NT 9.* WA 7 IV. 30 × 50 mm. Small fragment of a multicolumn tablet, reverse.
Left column: list of personal names with Sîn (ᵈ30) as initial elements; right column unidentifiable.

No. 26, 11 NT 6. WA 50*c* VI, pit (Fig. 61). 34 × 42 × 15 mm. Complete. Contract about the rental of a boat. Cyrus [x]/3/5.

> ᵍⁱˢMÁ *šá* ᵐ*Arad*-ᵈAK ˡúGAL.SAG(*rab ša rē ši*)
> NÍG KU LUGAL *šá ina* IGI ᵐᵈMAŠ-SU A-*šú šá*
> ᵐᵈUTU-MU-A *i-di-šú a-na* ITU
> *ù* 3 *u₄-mu a-na* 7 GÍN KÙ.BABBAR
> 5   ᵐᵈMAŠ-SU A-*šú šá* ᵐᵈUTU-MU
> *a-na* ᵐᵈUTU-ŠEŠ-MU A-*šú šá* <ᵐ>ᵈ[*x-x*-DÙ]
> ᵐ*Ta-at-tan-nu* A-*šú šá* ᵐᵈUTU-[   ]
> *u* ᵐᵈEŠ.NUMUN.DÙ A-*šú šá Ma-an*-[*di-di*]
> *a-na i-di-šú id-din*
> 10   *ul-tu* UD 6.KAM *šá* ITU SIG₄
> ᵍⁱˢMÁ *ina* IGI-*šú-nu ina* 20 *u₄-mu* [*i*]*t-ta-bal*
> *ana* ITU *i-nam-din ki-i* ITU 2 *u₄-mu*

*Tablets marked by an asterisk have only one side preserved.

> *it-ta-bal ša* ITU *i-nam-din*
> ^{lú}*mu-kin-nu* ^m[*x-x*]-*ga*(?) ^m*ra-di-ia*
> 15 A-*šú šá* ^dUTU-MU
> *u* ^{lú}DUB ^m[*ga*]-*gi-a* A-*šú šá* ^{m<d>}UTU-[*x*]
> EN.[LÍL].KI ITU SIG₄ UD 5.KAM [MU x.KA]M
> edge ^m*ku-raš* LUGAL KUR.KUR (and Aramaic) *lttn* (incised)

"The boat of Arad-Nabû, high officer and royal commissioner, which is at
the disposal of Ninurta-erîba, the son of Šamaš-nādin-apli, whose rental
price for a month and three days is seven shekels of silver, Ninurta-erîba, the
son of Šamaš-nādin-apli, has rented to Šamaš-aḫa-iddin, the son of . . .-ibnī,
Tattanu, the son of Šamaš-[. . .], and Sîn-zēr-ibnī, the son of Man[didi].
The boat will be at their disposal from the sixth day of the month of Siwan.
(If they take it for twenty days, they will pay for a month; if they take it for
a month and two days, they will pay (only) the (rent) of a month." (Witnesses, scribe, and date; for Aramaic see Appendix C).

For boat rentals in NB times, see A. L. Oppenheim, *Untersuchungen zum
babylonischen Mietrecht* ("Wiener Zeitschrift für die Kunde des Morgen-
landes," Beiheft 2 [Wien, 1936]) pp. 48 ff.; San Nicolò and Petschow, *Ba-
bylonische Rechtsurkunden aus dem 6. Jahrhundert v. Chr.* (Bayerische Aka-
demie der Wissenschaften, Philos.-hist. Kl., "Abhandlungen," NF, Vol. 51
[Munich, 1960]) pp. 48 ff. The interpretation of lines 11−13 is open to question and presents several lexical and grammatical difficulties which cannot
be discussed fully here. A parallel can be found in the boat rental contract
TuM II/III, No. 34:8 f.: *ki-i* UD 10.KAM *it-tab-bal* KÙ.BABBAR.ÀM 8-*šú* GÍN *i-
nam-din*. It would seem that, in the case of No. 26, if the boat is returned
before the 20th day of the rental period, the rental price does not need to be
paid in full; in the case of *TuM* II/III, No. 34, that happens if the boat is
taken only for the first ten days of a rental period of fifteen days. In both
cases the time during which a reduction will be granted covers approximately ⅔ of the rental period. In No. 26, there is an additional clause
which seems to imply a reduction of three days' rent, as a bonus for punctual
return.

No. 27, 11 NT 7. WA 50*c* V−VI, trash pit. 52 × 33 × 16 mm.; upper left
corner missing. Small fragments of envelope, not copied. Late Babylonian.
Findspot Achaemenid or Seleucid.

Letter from *La-ba-*[(*a*)-*ši*] to *Ni-din-tum*. The name of the sender is
complete in one of the envelope fragments.

Nidintum sends to Labaši 15 shekels of silver through Arad-Bêl. Three
soldiers have left in the boat of Arad-Bêl. The rest of the tablet is too broken
to get a clear picture of the remainder of the message.

No. 28, 11 NT 22.* WA 8, ancient fill associated with Wall C. 31 × 42 ×
15 mm.

Obverse destroyed; upper right corner broken off. Seleucid.

Administrative text; content uncertain.

Written after the seventh year (317 B.C.) of Philip Arrhidaeus (*Pi-li-ip-su*), mentioned on the tablet in an uncertain context (it is not the date of the text itself).

No. 29, 11 NT 10.* WA 8, north of Wall C. 60 × 52 × 21 mm. Left edge of a large tablet. Late Babylonian.

Administrative text; dealing, at least in part, with reeds and their prices (KI.LAM *ša* GI.MEŠ).

No. 30, 11 NT 11. WA 8, north of Wall C, in ancient fill. 17 × 25 × 15 mm.; fragment of upper right corner. Seleucid?

Administrative text; contents undeterminable; indistinct impression of one elliptic seal. Date not preserved.

No. 31, 11 NT 24. WA 13, southeast edge, ancient fill above Level I. 36 × 26 × 16 mm.; fragment of lower edge. Not copied. Seleucid?

Administrative text, contents undeterminable; indistinct impression of one elliptic seal. Date not preserved.

No. 32, 11 NT 2. WA 50c VI. 32 × 12 × 13 mm.; fragment of upper left corner, almost illegible (erased or worn out). Not copied.

Contents uncertain: IM and numerals (astronomical?).

II. INSCRIBED OBJECTS

No. 33, 11 N 191. WA 12, Room 2, Floor 12. Stone axe with lion. Fig. 28:3.

Two-case inscription: níg-ú-[rum] / ᵈnin-[x]-[(x)], "property of Nin . . . ."

On the opposite side there is an incised outline for an inscription, with the inside left blank.

The sign after nin in line 2 is almost certainly EZEN, although DUB and UM could also be considered. If it is EZEN, there is not enough of it preserved to determine the presence or absence of an inscribed sign. The mention of ᵈNin-gublaga (EZEN×LA, and variants) is not impossible; cf. Chiera, *Legal and Administrative Documents from Nippur* ("Publications of the Babylonian Section," VIII/1 [Philadelphia, 1914]) No. 13 rev. 10. The ᵈNin-ezen listed by Tallqvist, *Akkadische Götterepitheta* ("Studia Orientalia" VII [Helsinki, 1938] p. 402 as gír-lá é-kur-ra-ke₄, is in fact ᵈNin-mú; cf. H. de Genouillac, *Textes religieux sumériens du Louvre* I (Musée du Louvre, "Textes cunéiformes" XV [Paris, 1930]) No. 10:330, Urukagina 11:21 ff. (Sollberger, *Corpus des inscriptions "royales" présargoniques de Lagaš* [Geneva, 1956]), as well as An = anum I 328, so that despite the connection with the Ekur, this deity is to be excluded on orthographic grounds. According to a friendly communication from D. O. Edzard, during the 1973 campaign in Isin, the German expedition found inscribed bricks with a dedication of Adad-apla-iddin to ᵈNin-ezen-na, a late spelling for Nininsina, to judge from 12 N

543:13 (a catalogue of sag-gig incantations), which gives [én] ^dnin-EZEN ama kalam-ma, corresponding to the incantation, Ebeling, *Tod und Leben* (Berlin and Leipzig, 1931) pp. 156 ff. (DT 48 i 1 ff.); Wilcke, "Sumerische literarische Texte in Manchester und Liverpool," *Archiv für Orientforschung* XXIV (1973) 14, line 5.

No. 34, 11 N 157. WB 1/4, Level IV Court, Floor 1. Ceramic bead, perforated. Fig. 87:4.

The outer edge is inscribed with the following numbers:

[4]   6   9   11   13   16   18   21   23   [x] (see copy)

The series is formed by adding two and three alternatively to the preceding term, with the exception of the sequence 9, 11, 13, where two is added twice in succession. The inscription forms a continuous ring, and it is not possible to tell on paleographic grounds whether [x] belongs to the beginning or the end. The purpose of this numerical series is doubtful. Note that it does not go over the number of days in a month, but this may be coincidental.

The following tentative explanation has been proposed by Professor David E. Pingree. It assumes that the traces at the end are 2(!) and should precede the 4, and that 25 has been omitted accidentally (or for lack of space?): the numbers may record the last "full" day in a sidereal month that the moon is in each zodiacal sign; the last number, 27, would be omitted as unnecessary (on any day in the month above 25 the moon is in the twelfth sign).

ENDS OF ZODIACAL SIGNS	MEAN LONGITUDES OF THE MOON	DAYS	TEXT
	13;10	1	
30	26;20	2	[2](?)
	39;30	3	
60	52;40	4	4
	65;50	5	
90	79;0	6	6
	92;10	7	
	105;20	8	
120	118;30	9	9
	131;40	10	
150	144;50	11	11
	158;0	12	
180	171;10	13	13
	184;20	14	
	197;30	15	
210	210;40	16	16
	223;50	17	
240	237;0	18	18

	250;10	19	
270	263;20	20	*20 (text: 21)
	276;30	21	
	289;40	22	
300	302;50	23	23
	316;0	24	
330	329;10	25	⟨25⟩
	342;20	26	
	355;30	27	

The entries 16 and 23 are marginal; a strictly consistent scheme would have 15 and 22.

No. 35, 11 N 129. Surface of mound, near ziggurat. Fragment of bowl, translucent white stone, with a Šu-Sîn inscription:

ᵈšu-ᵈs[in]	Šu-Sîn,
[k]i-ág ᵈen-[líl-lá]	beloved of Enlil,
[lug]al ᵈe[n-líl-le]	whom Enlil [has chosen in his heart . . .]

Cf. *Cuneiform Texts from Babylonian Tablets in the British Museum*, Part XXI (London, 1905) Pl. 28, ll. 3 ff. (*UET* I, p. xxiv); J. P. Peters, *Nippur or Explorations on the Euphrates* (New York, 1899) plate following p. 238; *UET* I 80. Not necessarily a duplicate of either of these two inscriptions, since the formula ki-ág ᵈen-líl-lá lugal ᵈen-líl-le (ki-ág) šà-ga-na in-pà is too general and can be expected in other inscriptions.

No. 36, 11 N 128. WA 50c, Level X, 3. Fragment of a brick stamp, one half missing, baked clay. Sargonic.

[. . .]	. . .
[B]A.DÍM	builder
[É] ᵈEN.LÍL	of Enlil's temple

Narâm-Sîn: Hilprecht, *The Babylonian Expedition*, Series A: *Cuneiform Texts* (Philadelphia, 1893) No. 4, photo Pl. 2.

No. 37, 11 N 173. WA 8–13, under Temple courtyard, Level III. Small fragment of a cylinder seal, with the remains of a three-line inscription. See Fig. 30:3.

[	] AN.P[A(?)	]
[	] AN[	]
[	][x].LAGAB[	]

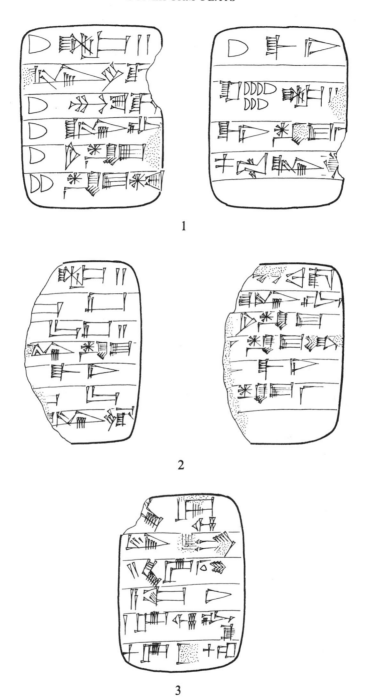

1

2

3

*The copies are the same size as the originals, except Nos. 13 and 14, which are ¾ original size, and No. 33, which is twice original size.

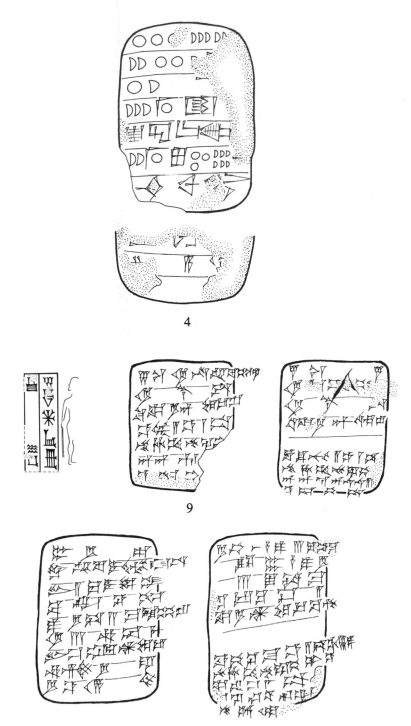

4

9

10

12

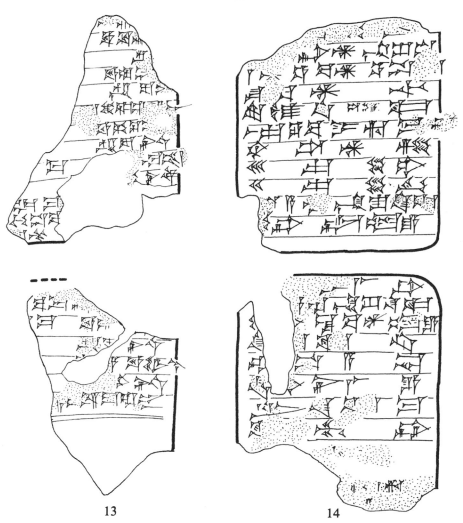

13 14

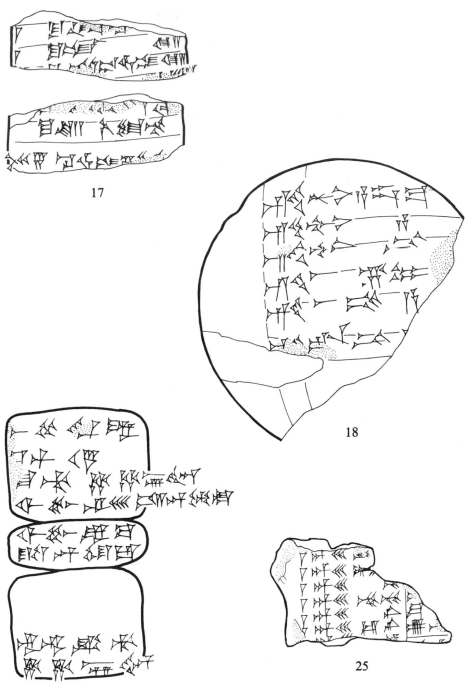

17

18

19

25

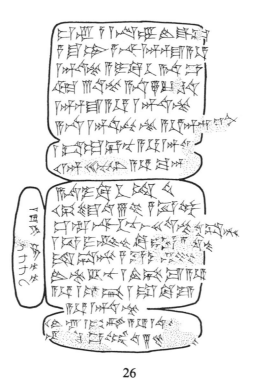

26

27

28

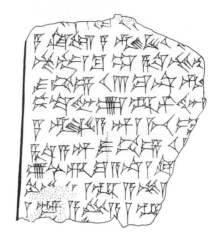

29

30

33

APPENDIX B: HIEROGLYPHIC TEXT

by Janet H. Johnson

Among the small objects found at Nippur during the winter season of 1972 was a crude Egyptian magical stele made of white stone. The bottom has been broken off in a fairly straight line, and there is a large fragment missing from the upper left corner. The preserved portion is 8.3 cm. wide at the bottom and 8.8 cm. high. The top is sharply curved, but it may have been flat in the center, for another, smaller, fragment, consisting of the very top and part of the upper back surface, is missing. On the front, carved in high relief, is a representation of Horus-the-Child, Harpocrates, shown nude, wearing the side-lock of youth. He holds a snake, a scorpion, and perhaps a piece of rope in his right hand; in his left hand he holds another snake and the tail of an animal. It is impossible to tell from the photograph of the object in its present state of preservation whether or not Harpocrates wore a uraeus.[1] To the god's left is the symbol of the god Nefertem; to his right the middle part of a papyrus stalk is preserved below the large missing fragment. Over the head of Harpocrates is the head of the god Bes. Bes symbolizes old age in contrast to the youth of Harpocrates[2] and was used as a protective figure at least as early as the New Kingdom.[3] There are nine lines of text preserved on the back and one column on each side, all part of a spell protecting against "those (evil creatures) who are in the water." Thus, enough is preserved to identify this as a *cippus* of Horus, or stele of "Horus on the Crocodiles," designed to protect the owner or user against scorpions, snakes, and other dangerous inhabitants of the water by means of magical figures and inscriptions.[4] Since Harpocrates, according to myth, had himself been protected from such creatures, it was felt that he was capable of protecting others from them. Many fully preserved *cippi* exist in collections around the world, by comparison with which we can restore Harpocrates' lower legs and feet standing on crocodiles.[5] On top of the papyrus stalk to his right would have perched a Horus falcon, probably facing toward Harpocrates. Most of the other *cippi* show Harpocrates, with the side-lock of youth

1. The original is in Iraq. This discussion is based on a photograph of the front and a cast of the sides and back. See Fig. 34:3.
2. Keith C. Seele, "Horus on the Crocodiles," *JNES* VI (1947) 44. Note the first two lines of the text on the back of the object, translated below.
3. See W. Stevenson Smith, *The Art and Architecture of Ancient Egypt* (Harmondsworth, Middlesex, 1948) p. 166.
4. For a discussion of the method of use of the *cippi*, see P. Lacau, "Les statues 'guérisseuses' dans l'ancienne Egypte," *Fondation Eugène Piot, Monuments et mémoires publiés par l'Académie des Inscriptions et Belle-Lettres* XXV (1921—22) 189—209, hereafter cited as *MonPiot*.
5. The major published collections of *cippi* include that of Cairo, published by G. Daressy in *Textes et dessins magiques*, Vol. IX of *Catalogue général des antiquités égyptiennes du Musée du Caire* (Cairo, 1903); that of the Walters Art Gallery, published by George Steindorff in *Catalogue of the Egyptian Sculpture in the Walters Art Gallery* (Baltimore, 1946); and that of Leiden, published by W. D. van Wijngaarden and B. H. Stricker in "Magische stèles," *OMRO*, n.s.

and uraeus, holding not only snakes and scorpions but also a lion and an oryx,[6] the lion by the tail and the oryx often by a rope around its neck. For this reason, it is suggested that the animal tail in Harpocrates' left hand on the Nippur *cippus* is the tail of a lion, and that the possible piece of rope in his right hand was around the neck of an oryx. There was probably a rounded, projecting base to allow the stele to be freestanding. This base might have had magical figures, words, or a short text carved on it.

Cippi are known as early as the Ramesside period[7] and become quite common during the Ptolemaic and Roman periods. In addition to the freestanding stele there are a few *cippi* which form part of a statue of a standing or seated figure,[8] and several small examples with loops at the top that were suspended and worn as amulets.[9] There are major differences between individual *cippi* in quality of workmanship, material used, and size. In addition, not all the elements typical of *cippi* are found on all examples. Some of the published *cippi* do not have the Bes-head; others do not have the staffs of Nefertem and Horus; on others Harpocrates does not have snakes in both hands. Sometimes all these elements are present, but the Bes-head protrudes above the top of the stele or the staffs are reversed or Harpocrates grasps the staffs as well as the various animals. Many *cippi*, although not the Nippur *cippus*, also include several magical "vignettes." Such variations reflect the craftsmanship of the maker rather than the age when it was made. But there are some noticeable developments in the *cippi* from the Ramesside age to the Roman period, including changes in the shape of the stele, the proportion of the elements, and the representation of the figure of Harpocrates. These characteristics afford a means of giving an approximate date for the Nippur *cippus*.

The earliest and latest are the most distinctive. The earliest, including those from the Ramesside period, depict Harpocrates in the pose typical of Egyptian reliefs—facing toward one edge of the stele with his legs striding toward the same edge while his shoulders are shown frontal.[10] The top is usu-

---

XXII (1941) 6–38. The abbreviations CCG and WAG are used in this appendix for Cairo Catalogue Général and Walters Art Gallery. Stricker gave a bibliography of *cippi* in *OMRO*, n.s. XXII 36–38, to which Adolf Klasens, *A Magical Statue Base (Socle Behague) in the Museum of Antiquities at Leiden* (Leiden, 1952) pp. 6–8, added more recent references. Mention is also made in this article of *cippi* published by Helen Jacquet-Gordon, "Two Stelae of Horus-on-the-Crocodiles," *The Brooklyn Museum Annual* VII (1965/66) 53–64; by Joachim Selim Karig, "Die Göttinger Isisstatuette," *ZÄS* LXXXVII (1962) 54–59; and by Werner Kaiser, the editor of the catalogue *Ägyptisches Museum Berlin* (Berlin, 1967).

6. So identified by Seele, in *JNES* VI 44, n. 13.

7. E.g., CCG 9403, 9413 *bis*, and 9427, as dated by Daressy, *Textes et dessins magiques*, pp. 13, 29, and 35, and by Lacau, *MonPiot*, p. 200, n. 1.

8. E.g., the statue of Petemios (Louvre 10777); the statue of Djed-Hor (Cairo "Journal d'entrée" 46341); and the Göttingen Isis statue published by Karig, in *ZÄS* LXXXVII 54–59. Both Lacau, *MonPiot*, and Klasens, *A Magical Statue Base*, pp. 1–2, discuss such statues.

9. Including those published by W. M. Flinders Petrie in *Amulets* (London, 1914).

10. E.g., CCG 9403. OI 10738, published by Seele, in *JNES* VI 43–52, has the face and shoulders frontal, the legs in profile.

ally fairly rounded. Several examples not only have a large head of Bes but also show his shoulders, reflecting the curve of the top of the stele (e.g., CCG 9405). The Bes-head occasionally protrudes above the top of the stele so that his shoulders form the top curve.[11] Occasionally, in the very early *cippi*, Harpocrates wears a typical Egyptian kilt (e.g., CCG 9427), but in most he is portrayed nude, as in all later examples. Dated examples of this style have been placed between the 19th and 26th Dynasties (1300–525 B.C.).

By the Saite period (664–525 B.C.),[12] there begin to appear examples on which Harpocrates is portrayed fully frontal, with face, torso, and legs all facing out from the stele. One leg is slightly in front of the other, as in Egyptian statues, but the god is always nude (e.g., CCG 9409). This frontal representation soon replaced the earlier "profile" representation. Some of the early examples with a frontal Harpocrates retain characteristics of the earlier style (e.g., Leiden A 1054, with a large protruding Bes-head whose shoulders form the top curve of the stele).

Examples dated to the Ptolemaic period have no striking characteristics. They are all frontal,[13] and most, but not all, have the Bes-head, usually within the frame of the stele. The Bes-head may be large in proportion to Harpocrates (e.g., CCG 9408) or, more often, smaller than in the earlier examples (e.g., CCG 9417). The top of the stele is usually less rounded than in the earlier examples and may even be flat with rounded corners (e.g., Cairo "Journal d'entrée" 46341, the statue of Djed-Hor, on which the Bes-head also protrudes above the top of the stele). In some cases the figure of Harpocrates is well-modelled with a thin waist and broad shoulders (e.g., OI 16881[14]), but in others the figure shows little or no modelling with no perceptible waist and no noticeable musculature (e.g., CCG 9407).

The Roman period examples are again quite distinctive. The original round top has either been exaggerated almost into a peak (e.g., CCG 9418) or become quite flat (e.g., CCG 9421), the Bes-head has been greatly enlarged (e.g., CCG 9423), and the proportions of Harpocrates have been distorted. He is now shown either very tall and thin (e.g., CCG 9421) or very short and chubby (e.g., CCG 9420), although still frontal. Almost all the published Roman period examples are quite crudely executed.

The frontal representation of Harpocrates on the Nippur *cippus* rules out the very early period, and the shape of the stele and normal proportions of the figure of the god rule out the Roman period. The very rounded shape of the top of the stele, the proportions of the Bes-head and the figure of Harpo-

11. E.g., the stele illustrated by B. H. Stricker, "Nieuwe magische stèles," *OMRO*, n.s. XXIII (1942) 13, Fig. 9.

12. Or perhaps earlier to judge by Brooklyn Museum 57.21.2, published by Jacquet, *The Brooklyn Museum Annual* VII 53–64. This is the lower portion of a *cippus* with frontal Harpocrates which can be dated to a King Osorkon.

13. The attribution to the Ptolemaic period of Ägyptisches Museum Berlin 1020, with a "profile" representation of Harpocrates, is probably incorrect.

14. Published by Seele, in *JNES* VI 43–52.

crates, the lack of modelling of the figure, and the general arrangement of the elements are most similar to CCG 9401, 9407, 9408, WAG 734, Leiden A 1045, 1046, 1053, OI 16881, Brooklyn Museum 60.73, MMA 20.2.23, L 10777, and Geneva D 1329.[15] Of this group, those that have been dated are either Persian or (early) Ptolemaic.[16] Thus, the Nippur *cippus* can probably be dated most safely to the late Persian or early Ptolemaic period.

The Nippur *cippus* also resembles the scene on the Metternich Stele, which dates from the reign of Nectanebo II, at the end of the 30th Dynasty.[17] This beautifully carved, round-topped stele, the fullest, most complete *cippus* preserved, contains a very large number of magical figures, several long magical spells, and, in a rectangular inset on the front, a typical *cippus* scene as well as other magical elements not found on the more abbreviated *cippi*. Three of the spells on the Metternich Stele are found, either in their full form as on that stele or in a shorter form, on a majority of other *cippi*. The inscription on the Nippur *cippus* is extremely badly worn, especially on the back, where the signs which are preserved look like stick figures and gouges. Whether they were as ill-formed when originally carved is impossible to determine, but in many places the signs are very crowded together, sometimes rather awkwardly. No complete line of text can be read from the cast, but enough can be discerned to identify this as the "B" text,[18] lines 38—48 of the Metternich Stele.[19] Once the text had been identified, most of the rest of the otherwise unintelligible holes and scratches left in the first seven lines and the beginning of line 8 on the back and the two columns on the sides could be read by comparison with published parallels.[20] Thus, even though the inscription is badly worn, the readings given here are certain unless otherwise indicated.[21] The restorations are based on the parallels mentioned earlier, especially the Metternich Stele and OI 16881. In the commentary only the

15. Brooklyn Museum 60.73 has been published by Jacquet, *The Brooklyn Museum Annual* VII 53—64. A photograph of MMA 20.2.23 is the illustration for the month of May in a calendar entitled "Ancient Egyptian Magic Calendar 1974," published by the Metropolitan Museum of Art, New York. Geneva D 1329 has been published by Campbell Bonner, *Studies in Magical Amulets* ("University of Michigan Studies," Humanistic Series XLIX [Ann Arbor, 1950]), Pl. 24, Fig. 5.

16. Except Geneva D 1329, of which Bonner, *Studies in Magical Amulets,* p. 157, n. 4, says "It is evidently contemporary with the Graeco-Egyptian amulets of the Roman period."

17. Published, with excellent photographs, by Nora E. Scott, "The Metternich Stela," *Bulletin of the Metropolitan Museum of Art,* n.s., IX (1951) 201—17.

18. So called by Daressy, *Textes et dessins magiques,* p. 12 *et passim.*

19. My thanks to Mr. David P. Silverman, who helped with the initial reading and identification of the text as Spell 5 of the Metternich Stele.

20. These are very numerous. The ones to which reference was made most commonly, in addition to the Metternich Stele, are Brooklyn Museum 60.73, OI 16881, and WAG 738 and 742. Steindorff, however, published only a translation of the spell; no photograph or hand copy of the texts is included. The version in OI 16881 is especially close to that of the Nippur *cippus*. The texts on the Metternich Stele were published, with translation and commentary, by C. E. Sander-Hansen, *Die Texte der Metternichstele* ("Analecta Aegyptiaca" VII [Copenhagen, 1956]).

21. I would like to thank Mr. Edward J. Brovarski for preparing the hand copy.

problematic restorations and the variations between this text and the parallels are discussed. For a fuller commentary on the passage itself, and for a translation of the portion missing at the bottom of the stele, see the publications mentioned previously. Since the text is quite "traditional" in spelling and grammar, there is nothing in the inscription which helps date the *cippus* more precisely.

1

2

3

4

5

6

7

8

9

TRANSLATION

1. [Oh ancient one] who rejuvenates himself [in] his time, ⟨ol⟩d man who
2. renews ⟨his⟩ y⟨ou⟩th, may you send Thoth to me at [⟨my⟩ cry]
3. so that he [may drive] back Grim-Face for me. Osiris is on the w[at]er; the eye of Horus is
4. [with h]im; the great Win⟨ged⟩ Disk hovers over him; the Great One is in his grasp

5.   [who bore] the gods as a child. If one approaches that which is on the water, one approaches the ⟨weeping⟩ e[ye of]

6.   [Horus]. Back, oh (these) water-dwellers, this en[emy], dead man, dead woman, opponent. Do not raise your faces,

7.   water-dwellers, until Osiris has passed by you. [He is (bound) for Busiris. May your] mouths [stop up], may your throats

8.   block up. Back, you evildoer. Do not raise [your] face . . . .

9.   . . .

9 + x   [Beware of repeating your injury a second time because of this which you have done]

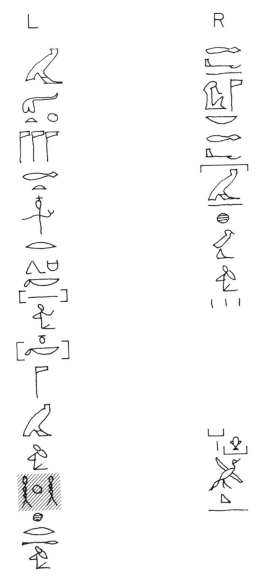

L   R

L. before the great ennead. Control ⟨yourself⟩, withdraw [from] me. I am a god . . . sound [of the loud cry since night began on the bank of Nedjit—the sound of the]

R. loud [cry] of all the great gods [mourning] at this injury [which the evildoer has done to you].

COMMENTARY

Line 1.—This spell should begin *i i3w rnp sw,* "Oh ancient one who rejuvenates himself." But there is room at the beginning of line 1 for only half a group. There is no evidence that there was ever a line above the present line 1. If there had been, one would expect that the division line would have been preserved, as elsewhere on the back of the stele. Thus, the correct restoration is uncertain.

The spelling of *nw,* "time," with the adze on the block of wood ⌁ just before the sun determinative is unusual but seems certain.

Lines 1–2.—The parallels have *nḥḥ ir ḥwnw.f,* "old man who renews his youth." There is room above the preserved *ḥ* for a second *ḫ* but no room for an *n* unless the horizontal sign under the sun determinative of *nw,* which I have read *f,* is actually an *n.* Nothing is lost at the beginning of line 2, where the scribe omitted the middle group *wn* from the word *ḥwnw,* "youth."

Line 2.—The parallels have *ḥr ḥrw.i,* "at my cry." The preserved strokes do not fit the normal writing of *ḥrw* but might fit the suggested spelling, which is based on the spelling found at the bottom of column L.

Line 4.—The spacing of the *f,* ʿ, and *y* at the beginning of the preserved portion of the line indicates that the scribe omitted the *p* of ʿ*py,* "the Winged Disk."

Lines 4–5.—The form *wrt,* "Great One," is, according to Seele (*JNES* VI 47, n. 44), known only in OI 16881. The variants have *wr.* But the reading seems certain, and the *m* at the end of the line is positive. There is room at the beginning of line 5 only for *msw,* "who bore." Thus, *ḫfʿ.f,* "his grasp," must have been omitted in going from one line to the next.

Lines 5–6.—There does not seem to be room to restore the full form *irt-Ḥr iḫ,* "weeping eye of Horus," which is found in the parallels.

Line 6.—The traces of *ḫfty,* "enemy," are far from convincing, but the reading seems necessary by the parallels.

What has been read as a *t* and walking legs after *d3,* "opponent," could be the head and feet of the determinative of the man with blood streaming from his head (⟨img⟩ or ⟨img⟩). Most of the parallels have both "male opponent" and "female opponent," but there is not room here for both. I cannot suggest what, if anything, is missing between *f3* and *ḥr.tn.*

Line 7.—The order of the determinatives in *imyw-mw,* "water dwellers," is unexpected but certain.

There are no signs preserved between *ḥr.tn* in the clause *r sšt wsir ḥr.tn,* "until Osiris has passed by you," and *r.tn,* "your mouths," at the end of the line, but [*(m) sw r ḏdt šr*] *r.tn,* "[He is (bound) for Busiris. May your] mouths [stop up]," as in the parallels, fits the available space quite well.

Lines 8–9.—Nothing is legible after *ḥr*, "[your] face."

Line 9 + x.—The restoration of the beginning of this sentence is taken from OI 16881, translated by Seele, in *JNES* VI 47.

Column L.—L is the column to the left of the inscription, R the column to the right.

After *ḥsf r* the pronoun *k* is needed in the phrase "Control yourself."

After *ink nṯr*, "I am a god," the parallels have *hy hy* (written *hy sp sn*), "hail, hail." I can account for neither the *m* nor the man with hand to mouth (𓀁), although both seem quite clear. I am uncertain of the signs between the latter sign and the word *ḥrw*, "sound." The group resembles *nḥḥ*, "eternity," written with the sun determinative between two *ḥ*'s. But it certainly is not, as in the parallels, *nn sḏm.n.k*, translated "have you not heard" by Seele, in *JNES* VI 47, and Sander-Hansen, *Die Texte der Metternichstele*, p. 34.

The restoration of the end of this column is taken from OI 16881, translated by Seele, in *JNES* VI 47.

Column R.—The restoration *m nhw*, "mourning," does not fill the available space, but I am uncertain what else to add.

The restoration of the end of the sentence is taken from OI 16881, translated by Seele, in *JNES* VI 47.

Because the amount of text missing between line 8 and the beginning of column L, as well as the amount missing at the bottom of each column, can be determined from the parallels, the approximate size of the missing bottom of the stele can be reconstructed. In the preserved portion only one clause from the Metternich Stele is omitted. It is possible that clauses were omitted in the missing section, but, if not, there may be as many as nine lines broken off at the bottom with at least as much missing from the bottom of each column as is found in the preserved part. Since the signs grow more crowded in the bottom half of the preserved text, this estimate may be slightly too large; nevertheless, the stele may originally have been almost twice as high as it is now. If so, the projecting base suggested earlier may have been rather high.

How this piece, certainly of Egyptian manufacture, came to be carried to Nippur cannot, at this date, be ascertained. Unlike some *cippi*, this one, at least in the preserved portion, does not name the person for whom it was made.[22] Thus, one cannot tell whether it was made for a man who might have gone to Nippur in some official capacity or for one who became a prisoner of war and was sent to work at Nippur.[23]

---

22. Examples of *cippi* bearing names are L 10777 and Cairo "Journal d'entrée" 46341, parts of statues, Brooklyn Museum 57.21.2, and OI 10738, on which see Seele, in *JNES* VI 49.

23. *Cippi* have also been found at Byblos, as noted by Steindorff, *Catalogue of . . . the Walters Art Gallery*, p. 163, n. 5, and at Hama, for which see Harald Ingholt, *Rapport préliminaire sur sept campagnes de fouilles à Hama en Syrie (1932–38)* (Copenhagen, 1940) Pl. 40.

APPENDIX C: ALPHABETIC TEXTS

by Stephen A. Kaufman

Magic Bowls and Fragments

11 N 78. Surface of West Mound, 50 meters southeast of WA 50c. Found very close to 11 N 77; perhaps from same room of a house. Fig. 89:4.

This complete bowl with its extremely carelessly written text in a large "Jewish" script beginning at the center of the bowl is significant because of its unusual list of maladies and because of the place name ʾyrg in line 6, representing the earliest known occurrence of the name "Iraq," here used in its original sense of southernmost Mesopotamia.

The following is a preliminary transliteration and translation:

1   mwmwmnw(!) ʿlykwn wmšbʿnʾ ʿlykwn ʿwbdy byšy
2   wmʿbdy byšy šydy šbṭy plgy pgʿy wryry rwḥy(?) byštʾ
3   rwḥ ḥwmry wrwḥ ḥršy kybʾ šbtʾ b/pḥytʾ ḥkwkʾ kybʾ
4   dmʾ wdmʿtʾ ṣwr/dqy wslḥtʾ wkl rwḥwt myštryn bḥršy byšy
5   wbmʿbdy rydwpy wkl kyby dkybyn wkl rmʾy trmn wkl rwdy tmwtwdwn(!)
6   ʾšbʿyt ʿlykwn rwḥy bbl wʿrb rwḥy ʾyrg wmyšwn rwḥy prt wdglt nhrh tdyzʿwn
7   wtslqwn wtmwtwn mn mʾtn ḥmšyn wtryn ḥrmy qymt ḥdḥdy ʾp mn dwdw bt dwdw
8   ʾmn ʾmn slh

1   I swear upon you and adjure you evil deeds
2   and evil doings, demons, plagues, headache demons, afflicters, eye diseases, evil spirits,
3   charm spirit and sorcery spirit, pain, wretched(?) Šibta spirit, scab,
4   blood and tears, scars(?) and migraine and all spirits loosed by evil sorcery
5   and by persecuting deeds and all painful pains and all deceivers; may you be cast down and all . . . may you die.
6   I adjure you spirits of Babylon and Arab, spirits of Iraq and Mesene, spirits of the Euphrates and the River Tigris, may you depart,
7   vanish and die by means of the two hundred and fifty-two bans (standing together?); even from Dodo, daughter of Dodo,
8   amen, amen, selah.

11 N 77. Surface of West Mound, 50 meters southeast of WA 50c. Found very close to 11 N 78. Fig. 89:3.

This text in the "Jewish" script, with a frightful demon depicted in the center of the bowl, is a partial duplicate of a standard incantation known from several other bowls (cf. J. A. Montgomery, *Aramaic Incantation Texts from Nippur* ["Publications of the Babylonian Section," III (Philadelphia, 1913)] No. 11). It invokes the name of Bagdana, king of the demons and great ruler of the Liliths, as an adjuration against the Lilith Hablas, who is described as killing boys and girls and snatching little children from the laps of their mothers.

11 N 7. WA, loose debris above Level I. Fig. 38:1. Fragment of a magic bowl inscribed in Mandaic script.

11 N 8. WA, loose debris above Level I. Fig. 38:2a–b. Fragment of a bowl(?) inscribed in several directions on both sides in a large, carefully executed, cursive "Jewish" script. No sense can be made of the isolated words.

11 N 9. Surface of West Mound. Fig. 38:3. Fragment of a bowl inscribed in "Jewish" script.

11 N 21. WA 7, fill in Pennsylvania cut. Fig. 38:4. Fragment of a bowl inscribed in "Jewish" script.

Tablets

11 NT 8. WA 50c, Level VI, pit. Fragment of an Aramaic tablet probably recording a debt.

1   lslw 'll   "To Silim-Enlil . . . ."
2   [   ][ql qy/sp]

The diagonal line in line 1 beneath the fourth letter is not deeply inscribed and is not to be taken as part of a letter. In any case it does not cross the horizontal, and if the letter in question were a *mem*, its right leg would point more toward the left. This Aramaic transliteration represents the well known Neo-Babylonian pronunciation of intervocalic *m* as *w*.

In line 2 the reading [x sql ksp] suggests itself, but the antepenultimate letter is almost certainly *q* and cannot be *k*. Compare Akkadian *qīpu*, "agent."

11 NT 6. WA 50c, Level VI, pit. See Appendix A, No. 26.

A brief Aramaic endorsement on a Late Babylonian boat contract, *lttn*, "belonging to Tattannu," i.e. ^lta-at-tan-nu, one of the parties to the contract.